Building a Better Life

A Good Lives and Self-Regulation Workbook

Pamela M. Yates, Ph.D., R.D. Psych
David S. Prescott, LICSW

Foreword by Tony Ward, Ph.D., DipClinPsyc

The Safer Society Press
Brandon, Vermont

First Edition

Printed in the United States of America
10 9 8 7 6 5 4 3 2

Library of Congress Cataloging-in-Publication Data
Yates, Pamela M.
Building a better life : a good lives and self-regulation workbook / Pamela M. Yates, David Prescott ; foreword by Tony Ward. -- 1st ed.
p. cm.
ISBN 978-1-884444-91-3
1. Sex offenders--Rehabilitation. 2. Self-help techniques. 3. Cognitive therapy. I. Prescott, David (David Francesca) II. Title.
RC560.S47Y383 2011
362.196'891425--dc23
2011037925

The SaferSociety PRESS

P.O. Box 340
Brandon, Vermont 05733
www.safersociety.org
(802) 247-3132

Safer Society Press is a program of the Safer Society Foundation, a 501(c)3 nonprofit dedicated to the prevention and treatment of sexual abuse. For more information, visit our Web site at www.safersociety.org

Building A Better Life: A Good Lives and Self-Regulation Workbook
$24 plus shipping and handling
Order #WP152

Contents

Foreword

The decision to commit yourself to the process of self-change is a tough one, and not one to be undertaken lightly. It is easy for all of us to resist thinking about our lives: what is going wrong or how we really feel about ourselves and other people. Being fully honest and self-confronting is extremely painful. It is much more tempting to stay with what is familiar. The problem for you is that the familiar path, the easy path, is a very dangerous one, both for yourself and for other people. If you are really honest, it is easy to see that it does not work to engage in sex with children or with non-consenting adults to escape loneliness, to avoid feelings of powerlessness, or simply to feel alive. It's ultimately a dead end. You now have a chance to get to know yourself much better. You now can find out what is behind your sexual fantasies and offenses and can grasp what things in life are likely to provide you with a genuine shot at happiness and a sense of purpose.

This workbook will help you on the journey to self-understanding and change. As you go through this book, you will learn about the ingredients for a better or a good life, and you will figure out how, with help from others and hard work on your behalf, to achieve these new goals. Make no mistake, it is critical to learn what situational and personal factors are likely to increase the chances for you to re-offend. It is important for you to identify your unique set of risk factors—have no question about that. But it is also important to set personal goals for yourself that aim at happiness and a richer, more fulfilling life. The authors of this workbook believe you can do both of these things at the same time. I agree with them.

I want to congratulate you in taking this step. If you put in the necessary effort, face your fears and doubts, and work hard on acquiring the skills identified in this workbook, I am confident you will be able to live a life that is more meaningful and less harmful to others. It is your choice. This is your chance to make things different, and better.

Tony Ward, Ph.D., DipClinPsyc
Professor of Psychology,
Victoria University of Wellington, New Zealand

Introduction

Welcome!

This workbook is about building a better life and achieving life goals that are common to all human beings. Sexual offenses often involve the pursuit of worthwhile goals, even though sexual abuse as a means of achieving these goals is unacceptable and harmful. In this workbook, you will learn about the relationships between what you want out of life (your personal life goals) and how those goals relate to your offending.

What Makes This Workbook Different?

In the past, the focus of most treatment programs has only been about reducing your risk to re-offend. Although that goal is essential, this workbook will help you to reduce and manage your risk as well as help you to have a good life—a satisfying and balanced life, and one in which you are able to meet important goals without offending.

Among other things, this workbook recognizes that people are happiest and most fulfilled when they are working toward goals they can achieve. People tend to have more distress in their lives when their goals are only to avoid bad things. People have less distress when they also actively work toward having a positive life. In this workbook, you will also find an emphasis on enhancing your motivation and your ability to work toward these goals. The goal is to help you to have a better or good life that is satisfying and that does not include offending.

You will notice this workbook requires many written exercises. You will need to work closely with your therapist and others involved in your treatment to fully understand and apply the material ahead. Your therapist will help you to devise the best plan for moving forward. This workbook deliberately involves reviewing material and moving forward one step at a time.

What Makes Treatment Work?

One thing is for sure: a workbook is only as helpful as the treatment program it is used in, and the work you put into both. It is important for you to work hard to develop the best relationships you can with the people involved in your treatment. Research shows simply having a good working relationship with a therapist improves how well people do in treatment. So you will need to work closely with your therapist and other people on your case management team. If, for some reason, you are unclear about what you are learning or the goals of your treatment program, it is essential that you bring these issues to the attention of others so you can work well together. It is the same with your community support team—your probation or parole officer, your community supports, your family, and any others committed to helping you.

As you work in treatment and through this workbook, you will probably do much better if you take regular breaks to review your accomplishments, no matter how big or small. Ask yourself: How is your life even a little better than it was this time last week? It is easy to list all the negatives. Finding and celebrating the positives is not only good treatment, but a good way to live.

You are in a treatment program because you want to change. While you need to be motivated to do this, many other people are willing to help you. You will also need specific strategies to make changes—motivation by itself is never enough. This workbook provides information to help you to explore and develop new ways of living, to achieve your goals, and to manage factors that might put you at risk to re-offend. You will be most successful at making these changes if you establish a solid foundation of personal motivation for change. If you are reading this workbook and you are in treatment, you have already taken that first important step.

CHAPTER 1

What Motivates Me?

Part of the challenge when starting out on any major changes in your life is to think about what those changes mean to you and to understand your level of motivation to make those changes. It can be easy to make a commitment to change but hard to find and keep the motivation to make the changes. Change is often hard, and your motivation to make changes will ebb and flow over time—this is natural for everyone.

The first part of this workbook focuses on your motivations for change, exploring *how* you might make those changes to your life and why. The purpose of this section is to highlight your motivations for change so the rest of your work in treatment will be relevant and helpful to you. You will also learn about different aspects of motivation as well as strategies you can use to keep your motivation high when things get hard.

As you go through this workbook, the most important fact to keep in mind is that genuine change comes from within. Although other people can help you along the way, only you can make the decision to change your life. There are many experts in the area of sexual offender assessment and treatment, but you are the only real expert about both the person you are and the person you wish to be.

Getting Advice

The above points are important to make because you may hear messages that suggest otherwise. For example, when you are sick, you visit a doctor who prescribes medicine to make you feel better. Likewise, when your car breaks down, you take it to the garage, where a mechanic fixes it. You may have heard others say things to you like, "You need treatment," and assumed that treatment is something that is done *to* you, like it is to the car. A more helpful way to think about change is to think of it as being like a weight-loss program. You can get the advice of many experts on losing weight, but it is you who must do the work to lose the weight.

Also, some of the advice will apply to you, and some won't seem important when you first hear it. It is the same in sexual offender treatment. Some advice you receive will be helpful, and some will not seem important at the time. More importantly, though, the motivation to carry through with either a weight-loss program or a treatment program has to come from within *you*.

There are different reasons the advice you get might not seem helpful:

- Some advice you get may not actually be helpful.
- Some advice may not seem helpful at the time, but will become helpful later on.
- Certain advice may turn out to be helpful later on, but it may be hard for you to see right now how it might eventually help you.
- Sometimes the advice you receive might strike too close to home—it might apply *too much* to you—and as a result might be difficult to accept or listen to.
- You may not be ready to change, so you might not want to hear the advice.

Treatment, like weight loss, works best when you carefully listen to the advice of outside experts, such as your therapist. Sometimes others who are further along in treatment can have good advice, too. Advice works best when you discover your own reasons to change. For example, your reasons could include: "I want to be the best person I can be," or "I am tired of living my life on the edge; I just want peace."

Ultimately, changing your life is your responsibility, even though the best circumstances for making personal change take place when you have the help, support, and encouragement of others. You have the right to change your life, the right to make things better for yourself and others, and the right to work toward having peace of mind. The goal of this workbook is to help support your efforts to have a healthier and more fulfilling life and to help build a safer community around you.

Motivation often rises and falls. On some days, it is hard to find your motivation, especially when other factors such as depression, anxiety, or frustration get in the way. It can also be difficult to keep your motivation when you face community identification as a sexual offender, or when you are afraid your family might find out the details of what happened when you offended. Sometimes something as simple as having a bad day can decrease your motivation. Feeling this way is normal. Everyone has moments when they struggle with their motivation. It is not easy to make changes in one's life. As a result, it will be essential for you to have a plan in place—a set of emergency instructions to yourself—for those times when your motivation becomes low, for *any* reason.

Motivation and change are made up of a number of different elements. Those elements are described in the next sections of this chapter.

The Importance of Change

The first step in making life changes will be to determine *how important* it is to you to make those changes. The first exercise in this book will help you understand your level of motivation. This exercise is not about whether you think you *can* change certain aspects of your life. This exercise, instead, focuses on how important you feel it is to make these changes. This exercise allows you to explore your motivation to change. Be as honest as possible in your responses.

Exercise 1.1: How Important Is Change to Me?

Please carefully think about and write your answers to the following questions. These questions explore how important it is to you to make changes in your life and how confident you are that you can make those changes. Think about genuine changes you've been thinking about making.

1. To start, on a scale of 0 to 10, circle how *important* is it to you that you make changes to your life? A rating of 0 means you have absolutely no interest in making a change and/or you have nothing you wish to change in your life. A 10 means meaningful change is the single most important goal in your life right now, and you are eager to get going. Please do not write an answer you think others want to hear. This exercise is for your benefit and no one else's.

0	1	2	3	4	5	6	7	8	9	10
Not at all				Somewhat Important					Extremely or very important	

2. List five reasons why you picked the number you did.

   Reason 1: ______________________________

   Reason 2: ______________________________

   Reason 3: ______________________________

   Reason 4: ______________________________

   Reason 5: ______________________________

3. Now, write down why you did not pick a number lower than the one you circled. For example, if you circled 5, why didn't you circle 3? Your answers will help you later when you are having difficulty with your motivation.

____

____

____

____

____

____

Look back at your answers. They probably contain some elements of *desire* (*"I want to"*), *ability* (*"I can if I want to"*), *reason* (*"I really have to change because…"*), and *need* (*"I need to change because…"*). These elements are called *change language*. Change language contains important clues to your personal motivation, and can be vital to your attempts to build a new life for yourself. They point to your *ability* to change instead of all the various *reasons* to change, which other people may have tried to impose on you.

4. Now, think about the first question a bit differently. What would it take for you to be 2 points higher on the scale? That is, if you chose a 5, what would need to happen for you to choose a 7 instead?

____

____

____

____

____

____

Look back at your answers. Chances are good they will provide some kind of roadmap for how you can move forward with your life. Your answers can form the beginning of a plan for taking action to improve your life.

Confidence

Sometimes people want to make changes in their lives, but they don't know where to start, or they don't really believe they can change. They may think they don't have the skills or the energy or the opportunities, or that other people would not support them in making changes. Because this thinking may slow down your motivation to change, it is important to think about how confident you would be when making changes. The next exercises will explore how much you believe you can make changes if you try to.

Exercise 1.2: How Confident Am I That I Can Make Changes in My Life?

1. On a scale of 0 to 10, how *confident* are you that you can make changes in your life by applying your full effort until you have reached your goal? A rating of 0 would mean that you do not believe you can make changes even if you try your best. A rating of 10 would mean that nothing can stop you from facing and meeting the challenges that lie ahead. Please do not write the answer that you think others want to hear. Write only what you believe to be true about yourself.

0	1	2	3	4	5	6	7	8	9	10
No confidence					Somewhat confident					Total confidence

2. List five reasons why you picked the number you did in the above scale.

   Reason 1: ____________________

   Reason 2: ____________________

   Reason 3: ____________________

   Reason 4: ____________________

   Reason 5: ____________________

3. Now, write why you didn't pick a number that is 2 points lower than the number you picked. In other words, if you picked a 5, why didn't you pick a 2 or a 3? Give this answer a lot of thought, because it will become important later.

   ____

   ____

Continued on next page

Look back at your answers. They probably contain some elements of desire, ability, reason, and need to change. Just as before, these answers provide important clues about your personal motivation, and they can be a vital part of your work to build a new life for yourself. They point to your ability to change instead of reflecting all the things that other people may have tried to impose on you.

4. Thinking about this question differently, what would it take for you to be about 2 points higher on this scale? That is, if you chose a 5, what, for example, would need to happen for you to be at a 7?

Look back at your answers. Your answers can form the beginning of a plan for taking action to improve your life.

Knowledge

Now that you've thought about the elements of *importance* and *confidence,* think about what new *knowledge* you can take away from your answers to the previous exercises. Anyone who has ever tried to change his life knows that it can be one of the hardest things a person can do. Often it is harder to *maintain* change than it is to first start making it. Knowing about your internal reasons to change can be very helpful when you have doubts about whether it is worth it to change or whether you can even do it.

Exercise 1.3: New Knowledge About My Motivations

1. In the space below, write what new knowledge you have about your motivation that you can use in the future.

Look back at your answer and see how it reflects some kind of desire to change, or an ability to make changes that you may not have known before. It may also reflect your reasons to change or your belief that you really need to change.

2. Add a check mark next to any words that suggest a *desire, ability, reason,* or *need* to change. Then, if you're already committed to taking steps toward making changes, put a star next to those words. All of these words point to your own unique abilities to make relevant changes in your life. It is possible you never noticed these abilities before. Be sure to work with your therapist on any parts of this exercise that seem confusing.

Ambivalence

People often feel torn in different directions about changing. For example, one part of a person may want to change, but another part doesn't want to change. In fact, some otherwise fearless people are downright afraid of changing or of having to work with others toward change. Many people have said it seems as though one part of them wants to live differently, while another part of them wants to be the same person they've always been. It is very common for people to feel conflicted about changing. This uncertainty is called *ambivalence*.

The following questions explore the various parts of yourself that are ready and willing to change. This exercise is designed to help you think differently about change.

Exercise 1.4: My Desire to Change

1. What are five ways you *desire* to make changes to your life?

    1. ______________________________
    2. ______________________________
    3. ______________________________
    4. ______________________________
    5. ______________________________

2. What aspects of your life are you able to change? Some changes may be impossible. For example, we may never be able to make ourselves extremely wealthy, but we may be able to become comfortable under certain circumstances.

    1. ______________________________
    2. ______________________________
    3. ______________________________
    4. ______________________________
    5. ______________________________

3. What *reasons* do you have to make changes to your life?

    1. ______________________________
    2. ______________________________
    3. ______________________________
    4. ______________________________
    5. ______________________________

4. What are the ways you might feel a *need* to make meaningful changes to your life that you haven't explored already?

    1. ______________________________
    2. ______________________________
    3. ______________________________
    4. ______________________________
    5. ______________________________

5. What things have you already done to move toward making changes?

    1. ______________________________
    2. ______________________________
    3. ______________________________
    4. ______________________________
    5. ______________________________

Weighing the Pros and Cons of Change

Sometimes it is easy to consider change in a broad or abstract way. It is easy for people to say they are 100 percent committed to making their lives better. But, when it comes to making those changes, people sometimes back off a little bit, or maybe a lot. It is a normal reaction. Change can be very hard. When people change, they have to face what they have to gain and what they have to lose. This section will help you explore the pros and cons of change for yourself.

To start, weigh the pros and cons of making changes to your life. These questions include exploring your reasons for *not changing*. These questions are here because it is important for everyone to take an honest look at their motivations in all directions in order to make the decisions that are best for them. Although we are clearly in favor of change, safety, reduced risk, healthy lives, and safe communities, it is also clear that your commitment to change must involve looking at all sides of the issues.

Exercise 1.5: The Pros and Cons of Change

1. First, make a list of all the *positive aspects* or *good things* there might be about making changes to your life. Changes should be something you want to make, and not just changes other people might be telling you to make. You can return to this list in the future if you are feeling down or unmotivated, or if your treatment program seems too hard.

    1. ______________________________
    2. ______________________________
    3. ______________________________
    4. ______________________________
    5. ______________________________

2. Next, make a list of all the *negative aspects* or *not-so-good* things about changing. This list will help you make decisions about your participation in treatment.

    1. ______________________________
    2. ______________________________
    3. ______________________________
    4. ______________________________
    5. ______________________________

To make sure you are considering every side of the issue, now try answering some slightly different questions.

3. First, what are all the *good* things you might experience if you did *not* make changes to your life, or if you did not participate in or finish your treatment program?

   1. ________________
   2. ________________
   3. ________________
   4. ________________
   5. ________________

4. Next, what are all the *not-so-good* things you might experience if you did *not* make changes to your life, or if you did not participate in or finish your treatment program?

   1. ________________
   2. ________________
   3. ________________
   4. ________________
   5. ________________

5. One more question on the pros and cons of change: In what ways would you be uncomfortable with making changes to your life? What would you have to lose if you were to make those changes?

   1. ________________
   2. ________________
   3. ________________
   4. ________________
   5. ________________

6. Are there other areas of your life in which you might feel unsure about making changes? What are they?

   1. ________________
   2. ________________
   3. ________________
   4. ________________
   5. ________________

Hope

Hope is a very important part of change. This section focuses on what hope is and how it plays a role in your life. Hope has two important parts: 1) belief that a goal is possible and 2) some ideas about how to meet your goal. Think about the following example:

> *A good example of hope comes from the life story of Nelson Mandela, the activist who has fought for the rights of black people in South Africa. Mandela spent 27 years in prison for opposing apartheid and for leaving South Africa. Eventually, he was found innocent and was released. He then went on to become the president of his country. While in prison, he and others performed hard labor in a limestone quarry. Prisoners were segregated by race and because he was black as well as a political prisoner, he not only received fewer privileges than others but had the fewest privileges of all the prisioners. He was allowed only one visitor and one letter every six months. Despite his harsh prison conditions, Mandela studied with the University of London through correspondence and received a Bachelor of Laws degree. He organized the education of other prisoners and engaged in spirited political debate about how to build the best possible future for South Africa. What is now South Africa's constitution is a result of Mandela's efforts, because he never doubted that a better future was possible. Throughout those difficult years in jail, Mandela personally worked to overcome incredible odds, and in spite of the horrible conditions imposed on him, he kept his hope alive.*

While this story may seem very far from your own life or from things you think you could accomplish, you can probably think of someone you know who did great things because he or she had hope and because that person found ways to overcome difficult circumstances. Maybe you, or someone you know, has done something similar. Or perhaps you have heard about someone like this in the news. We meet many people every day who have beaten the odds through hope and determination.

Exercise 1.6: Roger Finds His Motivation

Think about Roger's case and answer the following questions:

Roger was in treatment, and he found his motivation to change the night he was arrested for breaching his probation. At that moment, he realized he was responsible for his actions, and that his circumstances were not just the result of bad luck. He decided he would enter a treatment program and finish it, no matter what. He was hopeful about his future, and he turned his hope into motivation.

In treatment, Roger looked at himself as a changed man and decided nothing was going to stop him from staying changed. He maintained throughout his treatment that the purpose of his program was to help him stay changed. Even though his therapists and family doubted his commitment—because of the seriousness of his past crimes—Roger knew change was possible. He used the program as a series of steps he could take to make those changes real and lasting. Roger kept his hope alive. He knew changing his life was possible, and he stayed focused on making it happen.

Many years later, Roger was still offense-free. He built a strong, lasting, and healthy intimate relationship. He also found a job he loved and that he was good at.

1. What happened in Roger's life that allowed him to change his life?

____

____

____

____

____

____

2. What experiences have you had in your life that are similar to Roger's?

____

____

____

____

____

____

Exercise 1.7: Accomplishing My Goals

Think about your own life and about some of the things you have accomplished up to this point. It doesn't matter how small you think they are. Your accomplishments can include getting your high school diploma, getting a job, or achieving any other goal. If you have trouble thinking of something, think about what other people might have said to you about goals you've met. Maybe your parents, family, friends, or others have congratulated you on your abilities when you've achieved goals.

1. Write some of your accomplishments below.

   ____

   ____

   ____

   ____

   ____

   ____

2. What personal qualities do you have that made it possible for you to accomplish the goals you set for yourself?

   ____

   ____

   ____

   ____

   ____

   ____

3. What kinds of situations were you in when you accomplished these goals? What opportunities did you have or what help did you get from others that made meeting these goals possible?

   ____

   ____

   ____

   ____

   ____

   ____

4. What are some goals you have for your life *now*?

5. What personal qualities do you have that will make it possible for you to accomplish your goals?

6. What kinds of situations might make it harder for you to accomplish your goals?

7. What specific situations might make it easier for you to accomplish your goals?

8. How can others support you as you work toward your goals (without actually accomplishing your goals for you)?

____

____

____

____

____

9. What are some personal goals you hope to accomplish by participating in your treatment program?

____

____

____

____

____

10. How can others help you as you make changes to your life?

____

____

____

____

____

11. What are your personal qualities that might get in the way of your full participation in this workbook and your treatment program?

____

____

____

____

____

12. What is missing from your life that you want to have? This could be something you have always wanted or something you had before, but that you gave up on, for some reason.

13. What could you do to get these things in your life or back in your life?

14. What are you longing for?

Exercise 1.8: Where to Go from Here?

Now that you have looked in a lot of detail at your motivation to change, where do you go from here? This exercise is designed to bring the various parts of your motivation to change together before you go on to the next part of this workbook.

1. Look at your change language (your reasons for believing change is possible, desirable, and worth working for), and also the less desirable aspects you might face when making changes. Taking those factors under consideration, what do you think you will do?

____

____

____

____

____

____

2. What are some of the good things about participating in treatment?

____

____

____

____

____

____

3. What part of this workbook and your treatment program might actually be enjoyable or satisfying?

____

____

____

____

____

4. Why would other important people in your life want you to participate in this workbook and your treatment program?

____

____

____

____

____

____

5. If you gave up on this workbook and your treatment program, what would happen?

____

____

____

____

____

____

6. Of all the reasons you've explored in this exercise, what is the *number 1 reason* you should start and finish this workbook and your treatment program?

____

____

____

____

____

____

Please take a moment and draw a circle around your answer to this last question. It contains much of the internal motivation you have. It lists a great deal of the internal motivation that will drive you to be successful in this workbook, your treatment program, and your life beyond.

Summary

In this part of the workbook, you have explored the good and not-so-good aspects of making changes. You have explored your *desire, ability, reasons,* and *need* for change. You have had the chance to review many elements that would allow you to be more confident about changing, and you have explored many of your motivations for change. In the next part of this workbook, you will have the opportunity to look—in detail—at what your goals are in life and what motivates you to have a good life.

CHAPTER 2

Understanding My Good Life Plan and My Goals in Life

Part of this workbook is about understanding what is important to you and what you want to have in your life. Those goals are different for everyone, but people have certain goals in common. Together, an individual's goals form a roadmap for living, which is called a *good life plan*. This includes all of the things that are important to a person that lead them to have a satisfying, healthy, and balanced life. Sometimes a plan or roadmap changes over time. Sometimes a plan changes as a result of different life experiences. For example, some things that were important to you when you were younger may not be as important to you now. Or, those things could still be important to you, but you have given up on them because you haven't been able to make them happen. You still might want to have them in your life now, though.

The exercises in this part of this workbook are designed to help you discover what is important to you in your life and to understand your roadmap—where you are in your life now and where you would like to go from here. Later in the book, you will be working on understanding what happens when things don't work out for you. You will learn how to change your responses *and* those situations so you can develop a healthy good life plan.

Common Life Goals

Everyone has goals in life. For some people, an important goal is to have a family; for others, it is to be successful in their work. Many people try to achieve both goals, and some are more successful at this than others.

Although everyone is different, certain goals are common to most people, and those goals are described in the next pages. As you read the list of common life goals in the chart below, think about how important each one is to you *right now*. Don't think about *how* you meet these goals—which may be healthy or unhealthy ways—just think about which goals are important to you. The chart includes some examples of how people get these things in their lives. These ways are just examples and there are many more ways. Also, you will see some of the ways are healthy and some are not healthy or are harmful to you or to others.

Chart 1: Common Life Goals

COMMON LIFE GOALS	
Life: Living and Surviving	This goal is important to people who think about or spend time being healthy or making sure they are able to meet their basic needs. Positive ways to meet this goal: * Exercising * Eating well * Taking care of their physical health * Surviving in the world, staying alive and safe Negative ways to meet this goal: * Spending time looking out for threats to their well-being or safety * Being hostile toward others seen as threatening
	This goal is important to people who think about or spend time seeking knowledge or information. Positive ways to meet this goal: * Going to school, completing training, taking courses * Learning about themselves, such as in treatment * Mentoring others Negative ways to meet this goal: * Teaching children about sex
Being Good at Work and Play	This goal is important to people who think about or spend time trying to be good at work or leisure activities. Positive ways to meet this goal: * Being good at sports or hobbies * Being good at a job * Getting education or training to become better at a job

COMMON LIFE GOALS	
Personal Choice and Independence	This goal is important to people who think about or spend time being independent and making their own way in life. Positive ways to meet this goal: * Valuing personal choice in most situations * Making plans to meet a goal * Being assertive Negative ways meet this goal: * Controlling, dominating, or abusing others * Feeling that the world is a dangerous place, or that they have to "get" others before they get them
Peace of Mind	This goal is important to people who think about or spend time trying to be calm and relaxed, or trying to reduce stress and its effects in their lives. Positive ways to meet this goal: * Trying to reduce emotional distress or stress * Exercising or meditating to relax or stay calm * Trying not to be impulsive or angry Negative ways to meet this goal: * Using alcohol, drugs, or medication to relax or to cope with emotions * Using sex or masturbation to relax or to cope with emotions * Having sexual relationships, even with people who cannot truly consent

Continued on next page

COMMON LIFE GOALS	
Relationships and Friendships	This goal is important to people who think about or spend time with family, friends, or romantic partners. Positive ways to meet this goal: * Spending time with family * Spending time with friends * Wanting or having an intimate/sexual relationship * Supporting family, friends, or a partner Negative ways to meet this goal: * Being a member of a gang
Community: Being Part of a Group	This goal is important to people who think about or spend time being a part of a specific group of people. Positive ways to meet this goal: * Being or wanting to be part of a group with those that have things in common, such as a Lion's Club or the military * Doing volunteer work * Being part of their neighborhood * Feeling that a group is important Negative ways to meet this goal: * Being a member of a gang * Being a member of a man/boy love club
Spirituality: Having Meaning in Life	This goal is important to people who think about or spend time looking for a purpose or meaning in life. Positive ways to meet this goal: * Participating in religious or spiritual activities (e.g., church, sweat lodge) * Meditation or praying * Reading or studying spiritual materials (e.g., the Bible)

COMMON LIFE GOALS	
Happiness	This goal is important to people who think about or spend time wanting to be content or happy, or to experience pleasure. Positive ways to meet this goal: * Doing things that give them a sense of satisfaction or fulfillment * Doing things that give them a sense of pleasure (e.g., sex) * Doing things to get a sense of purpose or direction in life (e.g., work, friendships, family) Participating in treatment Negative ways to meet this goal: * Pleasurable but illegal activities, such as drug abuse or sexual abuse
Creativity	This goal is important to people who think about or spend time creating or trying new things or looking for excitement. Positive ways to meet this goal: * Trying new things they have not done before * Painting, building things, drawing, etc. Negative ways to meet this goal: * Trying newer types of sex or more exciting sex that end up in abuse

Exercise 2.1: My Goals

Now that you have read about goals common to most people, what do you think about these goals? How important have such goals been to you in the *past,* and how important are they to you *now*? For this exercise, do not think about whether or not you can meet these goals; only think about whether they are important to you. Use the following chart to complete this exercise. Place a check mark in each column describing how important the goal was to you in the past and how important it is to you now.

COMMON LIFE GOAL	IMPORTANT TO ME IN THE PAST	IMPORTANT TO ME NOW
Life: Living and Surviving	☐ Yes ☐ No ☐ Not sure	☐ Yes ☐ No ☐ Not sure
Knowledge: Learning and Knowing	☐ Yes ☐ No ☐ Not sure	☐ Yes ☐ No ☐ Not sure
Being Good at Work and Play	☐ Yes ☐ No ☐ Not sure	☐ Yes ☐ No ☐ Not sure
Personal Choice and Independence	☐ Yes ☐ No ☐ Not sure	☐ Yes ☐ No ☐ Not sure
Peace of Mind	☐ Yes ☐ No ☐ Not sure	☐ Yes ☐ No ☐ Not sure
Relationships and Friendships	☐ Yes ☐ No ☐ Not sure	☐ Yes ☐ No ☐ Not sure
Community: Being Part of a Group	☐ Yes ☐ No ☐ Not sure	☐ Yes ☐ No ☐ Not sure
Spirituality: Having Meaning in Life	☐ Yes ☐ No ☐ Not sure	☐ Yes ☐ No ☐ Not sure
Happiness	☐ Yes ☐ No ☐ Not sure	☐ Yes ☐ No ☐ Not sure
Creativity	☐ Yes ☐ No ☐ Not sure	☐ Yes ☐ No ☐ Not sure

Now look back at the list above and at the goals you checked off, and answer the following questions:

1. What goals were important to you in the past? Were there any you gave up on because you couldn't meet them? List them below and also describe why you gave up on these goals.

2. Which of your goals from the past would you like to have in your life again? List them and describe why you might like to have those goals in your life again.

3. What goals are important to you now? Why are these goals important?

____

____

____

____

____

____

____

____

Later, you will be asked to think about these goals and how they all fit together, as well as any problems you may have had in meeting these goals.

Ways to Meet Goals

People try to meet their personal goals in many different and personal ways. For example, they choose to either work for pay or to steal money so they can meet their goal of living and surviving. Having money allows people to have a place to live, to feed their families, or to just be able to survive.

Think about the goals that were important to you in the past and the goals that are important to you now (look back at the last exercise if you need to) to prepare for the next exercise. This exercise looks at the ways you meet your goals and it has two parts—one for past goals and one for present goals. Use the Common Life Goals chart to help you.

Exercise 2.2: Meeting My Goals

Meeting My Goals in the Past

First, in the chart on the next page, write three things you did to meet the 10 common life goals in the past. The three things you did to meet these goals can be things that worked for you or things that did not work (and they can be positive and negative). The important thing about filling in this chart is for you to think about what you did to meet this goal in the past, whether it worked out for you (or not), or whether it led to offending (or not).

COMMON LIFE GOAL	WHAT I DID TO MEET THIS GOAL IN THE PAST
Life: Living and Surviving	1. ______ ______ 2. ______ ______ 3. ______ ______
Knowledge: Learning and Knowing	1. ______ ______ 2. ______ ______ 3. ______ ______
Being Good at Work and Play	1. ______ ______ 2. ______ ______ 3. ______ ______

Continued on next page

COMMON LIFE GOAL	WHAT I DID TO MEET THIS GOAL IN THE PAST
Personal Choice and Independence	1. ______________________ ______________________ 2. ______________________ ______________________ 3. ______________________ ______________________
Peace of Mind	1. ______________________ ______________________ 2. ______________________ ______________________ 3. ______________________ ______________________
Relationships and Friendships	1. ______________________ ______________________ 2. ______________________ ______________________ 3. ______________________ ______________________

COMMON LIFE GOAL	WHAT I DID TO MEET THIS GOAL IN THE PAST
Community: Being Part of a Group	1. ______ ______ 2. ______ ______ 3. ______ ______
Spirituality: Having Meaning in Life	1. ______ ______ 2. ______ ______ 3. ______ ______
Happiness	1. ______ ______ 2. ______ ______ 3. ______ ______

Continued on next page

COMMON LIFE GOAL	WHAT I DID TO MEET THIS GOAL IN THE PAST
Creativity	1. ______________________ ______________________ 2. ______________________ ______________________ 3. ______________________ ______________________

Meeting My Goals Now

Now, for each of the 10 common life goals, write three things you do *now* to meet these goals. You can list things that work for you, things that do not work, or things that get you into trouble or that lead to further offending. The idea is to think about what you have been doing recently to meet these goals.

COMMON LIFE GOAL	WHAT I DO NOW TO MEET THIS GOAL
Life: Living and Surviving	1. ______________________ ______________________ 2. ______________________ ______________________ 3. ______________________ ______________________

COMMON LIFE GOAL	WHAT I DO NOW TO MEET THIS GOAL
Knowledge: Learning and Knowing	1. ______ ______ 2. ______ ______ 3. ______ ______
Being Good at Work and Play	1. ______ ______ 2. ______ ______ 3. ______ ______
Personal Choice and Independence	1. ______ ______ 2. ______ ______ 3. ______ ______

Continued on next page

COMMON LIFE GOAL	WHAT I DO NOW TO MEET THIS GOAL
Peace of Mind	1. ________ ________ 2. ________ ________ 3. ________ ________
Relationships and Friendships	1. ________ ________ 2. ________ ________ 3. ________ ________
Community: Being Part of a Group	1. ________ ________ 2. ________ ________ 3. ________ ________

COMMON LIFE GOAL	WHAT I DO NOW TO MEET THIS GOAL
Spirituality: Having Meaning in Life	1. ______________________ ______________________ 2. ______________________ ______________________ 3. ______________________ ______________________
Happiness	1. ______________________ ______________________ 2. ______________________ ______________________ 3. ______________________ ______________________
Creativity	1. ______________________ ______________________ 2. ______________________ ______________________ 3. ______________________ ______________________

When Things Don't Work Out

For everyone, no matter how hard they try, their lives don't always work out the ways they want or in the ways they planned. Certain specific problems can happen that are called *flaws* in a person's good life plan. Flaws are basically problems that people have when they are trying to meet their goals or situations that occur that can get them into trouble.

Chart 2: Common Problems Meeting Goals

FLAWS (PROBLEMS)	WHAT HAPPENS WHEN PEOPLE HAVE THIS PROBLEM	EXAMPLES
Ways to Meet Goals (Means)	This problem is about the ways people try to meet their goals—what they actually do that doesn't work or that causes problems.	* Being jealous or trying to control your partner to get intimacy or sex, but behaving in a way that pushes your partner away. * Getting arrested because you had sex with a child when what you really wanted was a relationship with an adult, but you didn't or couldn't figure out how to have one. * Stealing to get money to survive, but you end up in jail with no money. * Using sex or masturbation to cope with emotions like anger, but the relief only lasts only a short time and your anger returns.
Too Narrow a Good Life Plan (Scope)	This problem happens when people don't have enough goals in their lives—when they rely on only one or two things to make them happy or to allow them to feel good. They have a few things that are important to them in their lives, but those things are not enough. A good life plan that is too narrow often focuses on short-term happiness rather than long-term fulfillment and sustained happiness.	* The only thing that is important or the most important thing to you is sex or partying. * The most important thing is your wife or husband, but then your partner leaves you. * Wanting a good job, but being unwilling or unable to get the necessary education or training for it.

FLAWS (PROBLEMS)	WHAT HAPPENS WHEN PEOPLE HAVE THIS PROBLEM	EXAMPLES
Conflict Between Goals	This problem happens when people's different goals in life don't match up, or when meeting one goal means that they then can't meet another goal.	* Wanting a relationship with one person, but also wanting sexual freedom with other people. * Wanting to make money to support your family, but not wanting or being able to work. * Wanting to spend time with your friends but also wanting to hold a job (for example, staying out late the night before and not being able to do your job the next day).
Lack of Skills	This problem happens when people don't have the skills or strategies to do what they want in life to meet their goals.	* Wanting to get a good job, but not finishing school and so being unable to get the job. * Wanting to have a long-term relationship, but not knowing how to meet people or how to keep a relationship. * Wanting happiness and pleasure, but not knowing how to get those things except through illegal or unhealthy behavior, such as drugs and alcohol.
Lack of Opportunities	This problem happens when people don't have the opportunities to meet their goals because external factors prevent them from meeting the goal.	* Wanting to be with your family, but not being allowed to because of parole or probation conditions. * Wanting to get a certain job, but finding that no one will hire you. * Wanting a better job, but not being able to get the training or education you need.

Exercise 2.3: When Things Don't Work Out for Me

Think about the last exercises you worked on, and then look at all of the 10 common life goals and decide what problems you have had in meeting those goals. For each goal, mark those where you had problems with a check mark. Then, write a short description of what happened when you had that problem. For example, if you stole to live and survive, you would check off "ways to meet goals." Or, if you wanted to get a job but no one would hire you because of your criminal record, you would check off "lack of opportunities."

COMMON LIFE GOAL	Life: Living and Surviving
PROBLEMS (FLAWS)	WHAT HAPPENED
☐ Ways to Meet Goals (Means)	____________________
☐ Too Narrow a Good Life Plan (Scope)	____________________
☐ Conflict Between Goals	____________________
☐ Lack of Skills	____________________
☐ Lack of Opportunities	____________________
	____________________

COMMON LIFE GOAL	Knowledge: Learning and Knowing
PROBLEMS (FLAWS)	WHAT HAPPENED
☐ Ways to Meet Goals (Means)	____________________
☐ Too Narrow a Good Life Plan (Scope)	____________________
☐ Conflict Between Goals	____________________
☐ Lack of Skills	____________________
☐ Lack of Opportunities	____________________
	____________________

COMMON LIFE GOAL	Being Good at Work and Play
PROBLEMS (FLAWS)	WHAT HAPPENED
☐ Ways to Meet Goals (Means)	________________
☐ Too Narrow a Good Life Plan (Scope)	________________
☐ Conflict Between Goals	________________
☐ Lack of Skills	________________
☐ Lack of Opportunities	________________
	________________

COMMON LIFE GOAL	Personal Choice and Independence
PROBLEMS (FLAWS)	WHAT HAPPENED
☐ Ways to Meet Goals (Means)	________________
☐ Too Narrow a Good Life Plan (Scope)	________________
☐ Conflict Between Goals	________________
☐ Lack of Skills	________________
☐ Lack of Opportunities	________________
	________________

COMMON LIFE GOAL	Peace of Mind
PROBLEMS (FLAWS)	WHAT HAPPENED
☐ Ways to Meet Goals (Means)	________________
☐ Too Narrow a Good Life Plan (Scope)	________________
☐ Conflict Between Goals	________________
☐ Lack of Skills	________________
☐ Lack of Opportunities	________________
	________________

Continued on next page

COMMON LIFE GOAL	Relationships and Friendships
PROBLEMS (FLAWS)	WHAT HAPPENED
☐ Ways to Meet Goals (Means)	______
☐ Too Narrow a Good Life Plan (Scope)	______
☐ Conflict Between Goals	______
☐ Lack of Skills	______
☐ Lack of Opportunities	______
	______

COMMON LIFE GOAL	Community: Being Part of a Group
PROBLEMS (FLAWS)	WHAT HAPPENED
☐ Ways to Meet Goals (Means)	______
☐ Too Narrow a Good Life Plan (Scope)	______
☐ Conflict Between Goals	______
☐ Lack of Skills	______
☐ Lack of Opportunities	______
	______

COMMON LIFE GOAL	Spirituality: Having Meaning in Life
PROBLEMS (FLAWS)	WHAT HAPPENED
☐ Ways to Meet Goals (Means)	______
☐ Too Narrow a Good Life Plan (Scope)	______
☐ Conflict Between Goals	______
☐ Lack of Skills	______
☐ Lack of Opportunities	______
	______

COMMON LIFE GOAL	Happiness
PROBLEMS (FLAWS)	WHAT HAPPENED
☐ Ways to Meet Goals (Means)	______________________
☐ Too Narrow a Good Life Plan (Scope)	______________________
☐ Conflict Between Goals	______________________
☐ Lack of Skills	______________________
☐ Lack of Opportunities	______________________
	______________________

COMMON LIFE GOAL	Creativity
PROBLEMS (FLAWS)	WHAT HAPPENED
☐ Ways to Meet Goals (Means)	______________________
☐ Too Narrow a Good Life Plan (Scope)	______________________
☐ Conflict Between Goals	______________________
☐ Lack of Skills	______________________
☐ Lack of Opportunities	______________________
	______________________

Putting It All Together: What Is a Good Life Plan?

In the earlier pages, you read about the 10 common life goals that all people have. You have also listed your own goals in life—both those goals you had in the past and those goals you have now. When your goals are put together in an integrated and balanced way, they form a *good life plan*. A *good life plan* is basically a roadmap that each person has about all of the things he needs in order to have a happy and satisfying life. This roadmap also needs to include ways to prevent the flaws described above and, of course, also includes being offense-free and not harming others.

In this section, you will be asked to put all of this material together into a beginning understanding of the good life plan you had in the past. Later in the workbook, you will put together your good life plan for the present and into the future. But, before looking toward the future, you will need to understand what was important to you in the past and who you are now. You will look at those elements in exercise 2.4 in the next section of this workbook.

An example of one man's good life plan is provided here to help you understand how such plans come into being with the common life goals and flaws.

Chris is 19 years old. He grew up in a rural area. His father worked for an auto parts store and his mother was a part-time nurse. Both of Chris's parents had problems keeping their jobs, and when his father was not working, he would stay home and party with his friends. Chris loved and admired his father, even though he spent more time with his friends than he did with his son. As a child, Chris became interested in the same kind of music as his dad, and eventually got an electric guitar. He dreamed of becoming a musician, even though this goal was mostly because of his desire to be closer to his father.

Chris would have liked to spend more time with his mother, too, but she worked at night. Also, she seemed to spend more time with his sister than with him. This lack of attention upset Chris, and he began to break rules when he was 12 years old. He also became increasingly frustrated as he tried to fit in with others his age at school. Unfortunately, he wasn't able to get close to others. Not only did he get into trouble at school, but his behavior also made things worse in his family relationships.

Chris molested his 13-year-old sister when he was 15. After this incident was reported to social services, he was sent to a residential facility. He got along poorly with others there, felt depressed all the time, and longed to go home. After nearly two years, the therapists in the program felt that Chris had achieved as much as he could, and they discharged him to a group home for a few months before he then became a legal adult. The therapists' hope was that Chris would prepare himself for independent living in the community. Instead, Chris headed for his parents' home, and his supervising agency closed his case.

Chris lived with his parents for a while, but he could not get a job. His relationship with his sister did not go well, as she still felt hurt and upset by his abuse of her. He spent most of his days smoking pot, listening to music, watching TV, and thinking about whether he should try to get a job or go back to school. He rarely played his guitar anymore. By this point, his only goals were to feel good and to hang around his parents' place until something else came along. He was sad a lot but didn't really know why.

Chris was recently convicted of a sexual offense following an incident in which he rubbed the breasts of his sister's friend without her consent during a party at their house. He had been trying to get the girl to go out with him for a couple of weeks.

Chris's Good Life Plan

Chris's good life plan has focused mostly on the goals of happiness and relationships. He has tried to find happiness through seeking pleasure and sex. He has tried to meet his relationship goals by trying to get a girlfriend, by trying to get his father's attention, by trying to fit in at school, and by abusing his sister. To a much lesser degree, he has focused on being good at play, and on his personal choice and independence. These goals are very common among young men Chris's age. But Chris has attempted to meet these goals in ways that have led to offending and to life problems. Chris also has tried to get peace of mind by using drugs. Fortunately, Chris also has some strengths and talents. He is also young and has many opportunities ahead of him. Let's take a closer look at each goal and how it relates to Chris's life.

Life: Living and Surviving

Chris has had problems trying to build a life for himself. His work toward this goal has been narrow, taking place mostly in the moment and without a realistic plan for the future. Learning to play guitar is an excellent hobby but only very rarely an activity from which a person can make a living. In other words, Chris's means or ways to meet the goal of living is not very clear. He lacks the skills to build a better life for himself and has cut himself off from opportunities to do so. Also, he didn't take his treatment program very seriously, and he is now at a point in his life where he isn't sure what to do with himself. Furthermore, the way he is pursuing the goal of happiness (by smoking pot and hanging around at home) will make living and surviving more difficult in the long run. Happiness and pleasure are worthwhile goals, but in this case, the way he is trying to fulfill those goals is in conflict with his goal of life.

Knowledge: Learning and Knowing

Chris has not placed much value or priority on acquiring knowledge up to this point in his life. Education is only one of many ways to gain knowledge. But Chris has not helped himself by creating opportunities for gaining knowledge. For example, he did not learn as much as he could have from his treatment program, and he can't decide if he should get a job or go to school. All of this inaction means he will end up with few skills that can help him move toward other goals, such as being good at work. In the long run, Chris will have many opportunities for gaining knowledge, whether the knowledge is job-related, hobby-related, or something else. The key for him will be in creating the opportunities to gain the knowledge, and in being able to recognize those opportunities when they arise. Chris will also need help to find out what opportunities are available to him.

Being Good at Work and Play

Chris's work toward this goal has been very narrow. He has an ear for music and enjoys playing the guitar. This hobby, which can serve him well in tough times, can also provide fun in his life. Playing an instrument can create enjoyment and may also help Chris meet other people and pass time productively. Now that he is a young adult, he may wish to consider other leisure activities, as well. Because playing music is the only real hobby he has pursued, his options for the larger goal of being good at work and play remain narrow. Also, because Chris did not go to school with the goal of figuring out what he might like to do as a career, his focus in this area has been narrow, as well. This limited approach can create a conflict with other life goals, such as living and surviving (when one has little or no income), creativity (Chris's time with his guitar is a promising start, but not necessarily a true creative outlet), and peace of mind (not knowing what one will do for work does not contribute to any sense of well-being). Furthermore, a narrow focus on work and play will make his relationships with others more difficult (living in one's parents home rarely works for long after the age of 18).

Personal Choice and Independence

At 19, Chris has not had many opportunities to become fully independent. He spent much of his early life with his family. Now that he is a young man, he doesn't know what to do with himself. Because he is unsure, his most obvious act of personal choice was to return to his home against the recommendations of his supervising agency. His narrow focus on happiness and pleasure in that choice left him with few opportunities for truly experiencing personal choice or independence. Even in his recent offense, grabbing his sister's friend's breasts was a display of force (a type of personal choice or independence) instead of a step toward actually building a healthy relationship (a problem with the flaws of ways or means). Chris is at an age when developing a sense of oneself as capable of making healthy choices is extremely important. But making healthy choices has not been a priority for Chris. He lacks skills in this area, and he has problems with the ways he makes such decisions.

Peace of Mind

Chris lacks the skills for maintaining a sense of peace of mind or a healthy balance of emotions. Just as when he makes personal choices, Chris has not placed a high priority on the goal of peace of mind, except when he tried to meet this goal by using drugs or possibly having sex to calm himself down. Even these actions do not help him in the long term, as he still feels unhappy. He clearly has a problem with the ways he tries to meet this goal. Fortunately, as Chris begins to explore this area of his life in treatment, he will find many options for developing peace of mind skills.

Relationships and Friendships

Chris has suffered from the lack of important opportunities in this area in his life. In fact, he spent much of his childhood trying to be closer to his parents than he was able to be. Although Chris may now tell himself that such closeness will never happen, or that it is too late for such closeness to develop, family relationships *can* change and move in different directions over time. But Chris's pursuit of happiness through sexual offending will no doubt cause considerable strain in his family relationships, and will likely also limit his opportunities for other forms of socializing. In other words, Chris's pursuit of relationships and his attempts at happiness and pleasure have been in conflict.

Community: Being Part of a Group

It does not appear that Chris has prioritized this goal. Persistent drug abuse commonly results in being part of a drug-related peer group, and although Chris enjoys "hanging out" around his house, he does not appear to have a meaningful peer group. He tried to connect to a peer group in the past but was not successful (representing a problem with opportunities). At the present, he does not seem to have any real ways of belonging to a group or of being part of a healthy community of people who are similar to him.

Spirituality: Having Meaning in Life

Finding meaning in life does not appear to have been a large part of Chris's life until recently. Now he is sad all the time and he is unsure why. He has only recently begun to think about this goal (mostly while considering going back to school and looking for a job). One possible reason for Chris to find it easy to engage in drugs and sexual abuse may be because he has had little sense of meaning in his life. Chris's unacknowledged goal of meaning in life has been in conflict with his goal of happiness.

Happiness

Chris has tried to make himself happy by doing things that feel good in the moment but not in the long run. Smoking pot, hanging around, and even grabbing a girl's breasts might feel good at the time, but those behaviors can hurt others, and they are also hurting Chris. These ways of pursuing happiness make meeting his long-term goals nearly impossible. A person cannot feel good about his life or have peace of mind when his behavior gets him into trouble with the law. Chris has a problem with the ways he tries to meet this goal. Happiness is something all humans pursue. Chris can use treatment to develop new, more effective ways to be happy and to feel good, which can then last his lifetime.

Creativity

Chris has a creative side. He enjoyed playing guitar when he was younger. He has not actively pursued as much knowledge or experience with music as he could have, however. His pursuit of happiness and pleasure through drug abuse and sexual aggression has come into direct conflict with his ability to pursue music and other creative outlets. Notice how Chris became increasingly sad and unhealthy at the times of his life when he did not have a creative outlet.

Summary of Chris's Past Good Life Plan

Chris has not had the opportunities many others have had. At the same time, Chris has not given as much thought as he might have to what is important to him. While pursuing happiness and finding a girlfriend are common goals among young men, Chris has not prioritized other areas of his life that might have helped him to develop a meaningful and more satisfying relationship. For example, when a young man feels as though he has a purpose in life, has developed positive relationships, and is part of a group or community, it can be easier for him to pursue happiness and find partners.

Up to this point, the ways Chris has led his life have put his goals in conflict with one another. He has sought out some goals but has ignored others. He has hurt many people along the way and has created limitations on his own future. He also has a problem with the means or ways he uses to meet his goals because his actions and choices have resulted in harm to himself and to others, and they don't allow him to meet his goals in the long run.

Exercise 2.4: My Good Life Plan Up to Now

In the pages just ahead, you will be writing about what makes up your good life plans, from when you were younger until now. Don't think about your life in the future; you will work on that later.

For this next exercise, think about your life history and the goals and problems you worked on in the last exercises. This exercise will focus on what your good life plan has been, *up until now.* You will describe what you wanted in your life to make it a good and happy life, and what worked and what didn't work. Write your answers on the blank lines at the end of the questions below. Write as much as you need to, but make sure you stay focused on the situation, your goals, times when you met your goals, and times when you didn't. Use the questions below to help you think about your good life plans up to now and answer all of the questions. Use extra paper if you need to.

1. When you were very young, what were the most important goals for you to achieve in your life? What were the goals you had when you were a teenager? What goals do you have as an adult?
2. What did you do to meet those goals in each of those time periods? Be specific and give details.
3. What could you have done differently to help you achieve those goals?
4. Were some goals more important to you than others? Which ones were, and why?
5. What did you dream about becoming later in life?
6. What got in the way of meeting your goals?

My Good Life Plan Up to Now

Continued on next page

Next, for all of the 10 common life goals you learned about in this part of the book answer the questions in the following section. Answer each question for every goal separately on the lines provided after the questions. This may seem like a lot of work, but it is very important. Your answers will be the basis for much of the work that lies ahead.

Life: Living and Surviving

1. What did this goal mean to you at different points in your life?
2. How important was it for you to meet this goal or to have it in your life?
3. What would other people have said about how important they thought this goal was to you?
4. How did the importance of this goal change over time for you? Did it become more important? Less important?
5. Would you have liked to have had more of this goal in your life?
6. What did you do at different points in your life to meet this goal? What worked best? What didn't work well? Think about both the long term and the short term.
7. What did other people in your life, like your friends and family, do to meet this goal for themselves? How were their ways different from how you tried to meet this goal?
8. In the past, what went wrong when you tried to meet this goal?
9. How were others hurt (physically, mentally, or otherwise) by your attempts to meet this goal?
10. How was trying to meet this goal related to your offending in the past?
11. Did you focus too much on this goal, causing you to forget about other goals?
12. Did other people tell you that you focused too much on this specific goal?
13. Did this goal get in the way of meeting your other goals? How?
14. What got in the way or prevented you from meeting this goal?

____

____

____

____

Knowledge: Learning and Knowing

1. What did this goal mean to you at different points in your life?
2. How important was it for you to meet this goal or to have it in your life?
3. What would other people have said about how important they thought this goal was to you?
4. How did the importance of this goal change over time for you? Did it become more important? Less important?
5. Would you have liked to have had more of this goal in your life?
6. What did you do at different points in your life to meet this goal? What worked best? What didn't work well? Think about both the long term and the short term.
7. What did other people in your life, like your friends and family, do to meet this goal for themselves? How were their ways different from how you tried to meet this goal?
8. In the past, what went wrong when you tried to meet this goal?
9. How were others hurt (physically, mentally, or otherwise) by your attempts to meet this goal?
10. How was trying to meet this goal related to your offending in the past?
11. Did you focus too much on this goal, causing you to forget about other goals?
12. Did other people tell you that you focused too much on this specific goal?
13. Did this goal get in the way of meeting your other goals? How?
14. What got in the way or prevented you from meeting this goal?

____

____

____

____

____

____

____

Being Good at Work and Play

1. What did this goal mean to you at different points in your life?
2. How important was it for you to meet this goal or to have it in your life?
3. What would other people have said about how important they thought this goal was to you?
4. How did the importance of this goal change over time for you? Did it become more important? Less important?
5. Would you have liked to have had more of this goal in your life?
6. What did you do at different points in your life to meet this goal? What worked best? What didn't work well? Think about both the long term and the short term.
7. What did other people in your life, like your friends and family, do to meet this goal for themselves? How were their ways different from how you tried to meet this goal?
8. In the past, what went wrong when you tried to meet this goal?
9. How were others hurt (physically, mentally, or otherwise) by your attempts to meet this goal?
10. How was trying to meet this goal related to your offending in the past?
11. Did you focus too much on this goal, causing you to forget about other goals?
12. Did other people tell you that you focused too much on this specific goal?
13. Did this goal get in the way of meeting your other goals? How?
14. What got in the way or prevented you from meeting this goal?

Personal Choice and Independence

1. What did this goal mean to you at different points in your life?
2. How important was it for you to meet this goal or to have it in your life?
3. What would other people have said about how important they thought this goal was to you?
4. How did the importance of this goal change over time for you? Did it become more important? Less important?
5. Would you have liked to have had more of this goal in your life?
6. What did you do at different points in your life to meet this goal? What worked best? What didn't work well? Think about both the long term and the short term.
7. What did other people in your life, like your friends and family, do to meet this goal for themselves? How were their ways different from how you tried to meet this goal?
8. In the past, what went wrong when you tried to meet this goal?
9. How were others hurt (physically, mentally, or otherwise) by your attempts to meet this goal?
10. How was trying to meet this goal related to your offending in the past?
11. Did you focus too much on this goal, causing you to forget about other goals?
12. Did other people tell you that you focused too much on this specific goal?
13. Did this goal get in the way of meeting your other goals? How?
14. What got in the way or prevented you from meeting this goal?

____

____

____

____

____

____

____

Peace of Mind

1. What did this goal mean to you at different points in your life?
2. How important was it for you to meet this goal or to have it in your life?
3. What would other people have said about how important they thought this goal was to you?
4. How did the importance of this goal change over time for you? Did it become more important? Less important?
5. Would you have liked to have had more of this goal in your life?
6. What did you do at different points in your life to meet this goal? What worked best? What didn't work well? Think about both the long term and the short term.
7. What did other people in your life, like your friends and family, do to meet this goal for themselves? How were their ways different from how you tried to meet this goal?
8. In the past, what went wrong when you tried to meet this goal?
9. How were others hurt (physically, mentally, or otherwise) by your attempts to meet this goal?
10. How was trying to meet this goal related to your offending in the past?
11. Did you focus too much on this goal, causing you to forget about other goals?
12. Did other people tell you that you focused too much on this specific goal?
13. Did this goal get in the way of meeting your other goals? How?
14. What got in the way or prevented you from meeting this goal?

____

____

____

____

____

____

____

Relationships and Friendships

1. What did this goal mean to you at different points in your life?
2. How important was it for you to meet this goal or to have it in your life?
3. What would other people have said about how important they thought this goal was to you?
4. How did the importance of this goal change over time for you? Did it become more important? Less important?
5. Would you have liked to have had more of this goal in your life?
6. What did you do at different points in your life to meet this goal? What worked best? What didn't work well? Think about both the long term and the short term.
7. What did other people in your life, like your friends and family, do to meet this goal for themselves? How were their ways different from how you tried to meet this goal?
8. In the past, what went wrong when you tried to meet this goal?
9. How were others hurt (physically, mentally, or otherwise) by your attempts to meet this goal?
10. How was trying to meet this goal related to your offending in the past?
11. Did you focus too much on this goal, causing you to forget about other goals?
12. Did other people tell you that you focused too much on this specific goal?
13. Did this goal get in the way of meeting your other goals? How?
14. What got in the way or prevented you from meeting this goal?

Community: Being Part of a Group

1. What did this goal mean to you at different points in your life?
2. How important was it for you to meet this goal or to have it in your life?
3. What would other people have said about how important they thought this goal was to you?
4. How did the importance of this goal change over time for you? Did it become more important? Less important?
5. Would you have liked to have had more of this goal in your life?
6. What did you do at different points in your life to meet this goal? What worked best? What didn't work well? Think about both the long term and the short term.
7. What did other people in your life, like your friends and family, do to meet this goal for themselves? How were their ways different from how you tried to meet this goal?
8. In the past, what went wrong when you tried to meet this goal?
9. How were others hurt (physically, mentally, or otherwise) by your attempts to meet this goal?
10. How was trying to meet this goal related to your offending in the past?
11. Did you focus too much on this goal, causing you to forget about other goals?
12. Did other people tell you that you focused too much on this specific goal?
13. Did this goal get in the way of meeting your other goals? How?
14. What got in the way or prevented you from meeting this goal?

Spirituality: Having Meaning in Life

1. What did this goal mean to you at different points in your life?
2. How important was it for you to meet this goal or to have it in your life?
3. What would other people have said about how important they thought this goal was to you?
4. How did the importance of this goal change over time for you? Did it become more important? Less important?
5. Would you have liked to have had more of this goal in your life?
6. What did you do at different points in your life to meet this goal? What worked best? What didn't work well? Think about both the long term and the short term.
7. What did other people in your life, like your friends and family, do to meet this goal for themselves? How were their ways different from how you tried to meet this goal?
8. In the past, what went wrong when you tried to meet this goal?
9. How were others hurt (physically, mentally, or otherwise) by your attempts to meet this goal?
10. How was trying to meet this goal related to your offending in the past?
11. Did you focus too much on this goal, causing you to forget about other goals?
12. Did other people tell you that you focused too much on this specific goal?
13. Did this goal get in the way of meeting your other goals? How?
14. What got in the way or prevented you from meeting this goal?

____

____

____

____

____

____

____

Happiness

1. What did this goal mean to you at different points in your life?
2. How important was it for you to meet this goal or to have it in your life?
3. What would other people have said about how important they thought this goal was to you?
4. How did the importance of this goal change over time for you? Did it become more important? Less important?
5. Would you have liked more of this goal in your life?
6. What did you do at different points in your life to meet this goal? What worked best? What didn't work well? Think about both the long term and the short term.
7. What did other people in your life, like your friends and family, do to meet this goal for themselves? How were their ways different from how you tried to meet this goal?
8. In the past, what went wrong when you tried to meet this goal?
9. How were others hurt (physically, mentally, or otherwise) by your attempts to meet this goal?
10. How was trying to meet this goal related to your offending in the past?
11. Did you focus too much on this goal, causing you to forget about other goals?
12. Did other people tell you that you focused too much on this specific goal?
13. Did this goal get in the way of meeting your other goals? How?
14. What got in the way or prevented you from meeting this goal?

___

___

___

___

___

___

___

Creativity

1. What did this goal mean to you at different points in your life?
2. How important was it for you to meet this goal or to have it in your life?
3. What would other people have said about how important they thought this goal was to you?
4. How did the importance of this goal change over time for you? Did it become more important? Less important?
5. Would you have liked to have had more of this goal in your life?
6. What did you do at different points in your life to meet this goal? What worked best? What didn't work well? Think about both the long term and the short term.
7. What did other people in your life, like your friends and family, do to meet this goal for themselves? How were their ways different from how you tried to meet this goal?
8. In the past, what went wrong when you tried to meet this goal?
9. How were others hurt (physically, mentally, or otherwise) by your attempts to meet this goal?
10. How was trying to meet this goal related to your offending in the past?
11. Did you focus too much on this goal, causing you to forget about other goals?
12. Did other people tell you that you focused too much on this specific goal?
13. Did this goal get in the way of meeting your other goals? How?
14. What got in the way or prevented you from meeting this goal?

____

____

____

____

____

____

____

Exercise 2.5: My Goals and My Treatment Plan

Now that you are in a treatment program, you will have a treatment plan that you would have worked on with your therapist. This plan will include a lot of things such as understanding your risk factors and the skills you will need to develop for the future. Looking at your life goals, what would you add or be sure to include in your treatment that will help you to meet your goals and to later develop your good life plan? This is about looking forward to what you want to accomplish in treatment and in going through this workbook. Do this for each of the 10 common life goals.

COMMON LIFE GOAL	WHAT I WANT TO ACCOMPLISH IN TREATMENT
Life: Living and Surviving	1. ______________ ______________ 2. ______________ ______________ 3. ______________ ______________
Knowledge: Learning and Knowing	1. ______________ ______________ 2. ______________ ______________ 3. ______________ ______________

COMMON LIFE GOAL	WHAT I WANT TO ACCOMPLISH IN TREATMENT
Being Good at Work and Play	1. ____________________ ____________________ 2. ____________________ ____________________ 3. ____________________ ____________________
Personal Choice and Independence	1. ____________________ ____________________ 2. ____________________ ____________________ 3. ____________________ ____________________
Peace of Mind	1. ____________________ ____________________ 2. ____________________ ____________________ 3. ____________________ ____________________

Continued on next page

COMMON LIFE GOAL	WHAT I WANT TO ACCOMPLISH IN TREATMENT
Relationships and Friendships	1. ________________ ________________ 2. ________________ ________________ 3. ________________ ________________
Community: Being Part of a Group	1. ________________ ________________ 2. ________________ ________________ 3. ________________ ________________
Spirituality: Having Meaning in Life	1. ________________ ________________ 2. ________________ ________________ 3. ________________ ________________

COMMON LIFE GOAL	WHAT I WANT TO ACCOMPLISH IN TREATMENT
Happiness	1. ____________________ ____________________ 2. ____________________ ____________________ 3. ____________________ ____________________
Creativity	1. ____________________ ____________________ 2. ____________________ ____________________ 3. ____________________ ____________________

Congratulations on completing this exercise! You will return to your answers to develop a good life plan later in this workbook. In the meantime, please write some thoughts about how you will use what you have learned so far until you have developed a more complete good life plan:

____

____

____

____

____

____

Continued on next page

Summary

In this part of the workbook, you have covered very important ground. You have learned about the 10 common life goals, and have explored their role in your life. You have looked at how important each of these goals has been in your past and up to now. You have explored how you have tried to meet these goals, and what has happened when things did not work out. This includes problems with the way you have tried to meet goals, narrow good life plans, conflicts between goals, and problems based on a lack of the right skills and opportunities. The next part of the workbook focuses on understanding self-regulation, which has an impact on meeting goals and on life problems and offending.

CHAPTER 3

Self-Regulation: Understanding How People Manage Themselves and Their Behavior

Self-regulation refers to how people manage themselves in specific situations; it includes *behavior, beliefs, thoughts, emotions, reactions,* and *perceptions.* Self-regulation is about how people respond to events that happen in day-to-day life, and how they make decisions about what to do in those situations. People's responses to day-to-day events are based on different factors, such as:

- **What is happening in the situation:** The same situation can provoke different responses in different people, depending on such things as each person's mood or beliefs. Different situations can also provoke different responses based on what is happening in the situation.

- **How the person perceives or interprets what is happening in the situation:** Much of how a person responds in a situation is based on how he interprets what is happening, even more than on the situation itself. People have "filters" or "mental shortcuts" called *cognitive schemas* that guide what the situation means to them, especially when the situation or the best way to respond is unclear.

- **How the person feels about other people in the situation:** A person's behavior, thoughts, and reactions can be different depending upon the relationships they have with other people in the situation, such as whether or not the person reacting likes the other person in the situation.

- **The way the person thinks, both in general and in that type of situation:** No two people think in exactly the same way, so different people often react very differently to the same situation. The way people think affects how they perceive the situation.

- **How the person usually reacts or responds in that type of situation:** People usually have patterns to the ways they react. For example, some people's pattern is to be spontaneous or impulsive, while other people tend to plan things carefully. Even for the same person, sometimes he will react impulsively in one situation, but plan much more in a different situation.
- **What the person believes:** What the person believes about himself, about other people, and about the world in general affects how he responds to a situation.
- **What the person believes other people are thinking about him, or what he thinks about others' motives:** A person is more likely to react in a negative way if he is suspicious of other people in the situation. A person is more likely to understand what someone else is going through if he likes that person or that person reminds him of someone he loves.
- **The person's attitudes about himself, others, and the world around him:** A person's attitudes and beliefs serve as "filters" for information in a specific situation. Those filters can cause the person to take mental shortcuts without thinking through the situation carefully.
- **The person's emotional state:** Situations can be perceived differently when a person is happy, sad, depressed, or angry. Different situations can provoke different emotional reactions, which then affect how the person thinks, behaves, and reacts.
- **The person's past history:** A person's past experiences strongly affect how they respond to situations in the present.
- **The person's expectations or concerns about what others will think about him:** People respond in situations based on what they think is expected of them or how they think others will see them. If a person is worried about what his family or friends might think, or if he is worried he will be judged, he is likely to disclose much less information.

People react in different ways to the situations around them, depending on all these factors. Reactions are different for everyone. Sometimes a person's reaction is drawn from a *combination* of the factors listed above, rather than from any single factor. This can cause a person to have trouble responding appropriately to a situation. For example, a person who is able to keep calm in most situations may become enraged when driving in traffic. His reaction comes from a combination of his circumstances, beliefs, and attitudes about driving, as well as from his tolerance for aggression. All of those factors make the difference between whether he manages his behavior or gives in to "road rage." People's brain activity and physiology contribute in ways that are not completely understood. Some people are better at slowing their reactions down and choosing how they respond to circumstances. Others find they have to learn and practice ways of keeping calm at all times.

Cognitive Schemas

In treatment, you may have learned about *cognitive schemas*. These schemas are sets of beliefs and attitudes that help people to understand and organize what is going on around them. They are used because too much is happening at the same time for a person to fully pay attention to everything at once. *Many* events happen at the very same time to people in their everyday lives. So many things happen at once that each individual cannot possibly think about or even be fully aware of all of these things while the events are happening. Because of this load of information coming in at once, the mind takes *shortcuts* to filter the incoming information so the person can make decisions quickly and easily without losing time or taking a lot of energy. If each person had to be aware of and think about every small thing he sees, hears, and does each day, he would never get anything done. Too much information comes at each of us, all the time, to think about a situation in that level of detail.

For example, imagine if you are at a job where you have to hammer two pieces of wood together with a nail. If you had to think about what a hammer is, which end of it to use, what a nail is, which end of the nail to strike, where the wood is each time you hit the nail, which muscles you need to engage so you can raise and lower your arm each time, how to focus your eyes on both the nail and the hammer simultaneously, and when you have hit the nail deeply enough into the wood so that you can stop hammering, the job could take all day! But, your "hammer-and-nail" schema allows you to do the job with almost no thought.

Much like the "hammer-and-nail" schema, if you believe someone doesn't like you, the shortcut you'll apply is to be suspicious about what that person is doing or saying, and perhaps to even be angry about what he says or does. Your interpretation of the person's behavior is determined by your past experiences with that person. Or, the person may remind you of someone else whom you don't like or don't trust. The schemas you apply come from the collection of beliefs you have about not being able to trust that person or type of person. When you believe others are not trustworthy, it becomes easy to have this attitude about them all the time. Such a reaction toward another person can happen even if that person was actually trying to be helpful to you. But because you don't like the person and you have pre-formed thoughts about him or her, you automatically think that the person is trying to do something bad or mean to you.

As another example, consider the phrase "authority figure." It can refer to police officers, judges, prison guards, and even psychologists, teachers, and social workers. Each of these titles means different things, and each of these jobs has a complicated set of responsibilities. If we had to think about these complicated responsibilities every time we encountered these people, we would become overwhelmed. For example, imagine that a police car pulls you over on the highway. Your first thought will be that this is an authority figure. Based on your own personal experiences, an authority figure will have a meaning for you that is also linked to your own memories, thoughts, and emotions. It is unlikely you will have much time to think about the police officer as a person, or to imagine the various daily challenges a police officer faces. You may think about these things after the traffic stop is over. But, in the moment you are pulled over, you will mostly be thinking the police officer is an authority figure, and you will be processing whatever that authority figure might mean to you. It is the authority figure schema you hold about police officers that will determine, to some extent, how you behave in the situation. That schema could also affect how you behave and respond for the next several hours.

In addition to thinking automatically and taking shortcuts, people also ignore evidence that goes against their pre-formed ideas and attitudes, because this information does not fit with what they already believe. For example, if you believe another person cannot be trusted, it is easy for you to find proof they are not trustworthy. It is much harder to see or accept that the person could probably be trusted some of the time. This response is simply part of how the human mind works unless we consciously do something to change it. The mind will always take shortcuts; it is how people survive. We cannot change our past experiences, but we can change our reactions to those experiences. Our shortcuts are based on our life experiences, how we feel about those experiences, and what we believe to be true. Schemas can be changed by looking at them, by examining what the evidence is for them, and by looking for different evidence and reasons the schemas might not be accurate. Once you change a schema, you can then respond differently to situations through that new schema.

Cognitive Distortions

You may have heard the terms *cognitive distortion* or *thinking error* in treatment. Those terms are often mistakenly applied to the kinds of thought patterns described on the previous pages. But, cognitive distortions refer to the assessments and judgments people make in a situation *as it is happening*. For example, some people often judge a situation as being more or less important than it actually is. Others judge people based on things such as their appearance or behavior. By contrast, people's schemas reflect the broader ways people look at the world and at their roles in it. Cognitive distortions are only a small part of those schemas; they occur in the immediate situation or in the moment. Cognitive distortions are the things that people tell themselves in a situation to make themselves feel okay about their reactions and behavior.

Cognitive distortions include underestimating the amount of influence you have over others, for example, "How could she be upset by what I said? She doesn't even know me"; or being wrong about how your actions affect others, for example, "My relationship with the boy is helpful to him. I'm not hurting him." Cognitive distortions/thinking errors can also include incorrect assessments of others and of their intentions, for example, "She has dated lots of guys, so she must really want sex." Here's another example, "That little boy really seems to like me. He must really appreciate the guidance I give him, and he's so curious about everything. That means it's okay if I show him what sex is all about."

Notice that these examples have to do with specific circumstances. They can reflect deeper underlying schemas, such as, "Children can consent to sex"; or "Some women ask for what they get because of the way they act or dress." Most people who see that a child enjoys spending time with them will interpret that situation as one of trust and acceptance of adult responsibility. Their schema tends to be that adults have a responsibility to keep children safe and to protect them. On the other hand, people who believe that children can consent to sex interpret a child's enjoyment of their company as a sign of sexual interest. Seeing the child's enjoyment through this schema, it is easy to forget the harm and the unacceptable risks to the child's life that sexual behavior toward them causes. It is also easy to misinterpret signs such as the child's silence as "evidence" that the child is okay with what is happening and that it is not harmful to the child.

The Effects of Schemas

Okay, so what do schemas have to do with self-regulation and with how people respond to situations? People with various schemas can look at events in their world very differently. A person with a schema that tells him he is not a good man will interact with the world very differently from someone who believes he is basically okay. For example, if a person believes no one understands him except for children, he will interact very differently with both adults and children than someone who believes he can appropriately interact with people of all ages. If a person has a schema that tells him authority figures are hostile and punitive, he will probably respond very differently to the traffic stop described earlier than the person who has a schema that tells them authority figures should be treated with respect and that they're just doing their jobs to help make the community safer.

How a person sees a situation depends more on his perceptions and beliefs than on what is actually happening. Sometimes, a person might automatically be angry or aggressive in a certain situation because of what he believes. His interpretation affects what he does in the situation. Here is an example:

As a very young boy, Mark lived with his mother. She got involved in a number of relationships, and it always seemed that each one of them became violent. Mark watched as his mother was beaten and often sexually assaulted. This dynamic became the way in which Mark interpreted relationships for many years. He developed schemas such as the belief that women deserve and want to be abused, and that men need to keep women "in their place." He also developed schemas involving the belief that men have to fight to gain respect, and that getting even with others is a normal part of life. Mark became increasingly hostile as he grew older, and he then became a pimp. He treated women mercilessly, and would frequently sexually assault them to remind them that he was in charge. His sexual fantasy life always involved rough and sometimes brutal sex.

In this example, the early messages Mark interpreted from adults' behavior—that men are brutal and women want and deserve the violence they receive—became a lens through which he viewed his world. He came to believe this attitude was true—his mental shortcut. Throughout his life, he never completely examined this belief, or he would have found evidence that his belief was not true. In fact, he was so convinced of his belief that he would not have taken any evidence against it seriously. This is how schemas work until people change them. Many people who have had abusive childhoods come to understand and believe that abuse is not okay, but this conclusion is not one Mark has reached yet. Furthermore, holding on to this schema allowed Mark to justify doing as he pleased with women, to not evaluate his actions, and to not even see his behavior's effect on others.

Here is another example:

Ali grew up in a family in which his parents did not trust authority. They believed anyone in a uniform was untrustworthy and probably dangerous. As a young boy, seeing his father arrested, Ali came to the conclusion that his parents were right about authority. Later, when Ali himself was arrested, he had a deep suspicion of the legal system in general. Today, Ali has a very difficult time trusting the prison staff and even his therapist, who is trying to help Ali. Ali wants to build a better life for himself, but he finds it very hard to trust any of the people with whom he works. He feels two ways about being in treatment. Every time a uniformed staff member walks near him, he feels both anger and panic.

Ali's life experiences with his parents resulted in his not being able to trust authority figures later in his life. His mistrust continues today, with his lack of trust in the prison staff and his therapist. This schema affects how Ali sees them, even if they are trying to help him. Ali also has a negative emotional response to the prison staff, so his schema affects his emotions, too. This schema also affects his ability to benefit from other types of help and treatment. If he does not trust his treatment providers because of his schema, he will not be able to let them help him, and he will not be able to talk about the things he needs to do in order to make progress in treatment. Ali will also probably become very frustrated in these situations, and, as a result, he might drop out of treatment.

Types of Schemas

Here are some examples of schemas that sexual offenders often have. These examples are taken from research studies:

- **Children Are Sexual Objects**. This is the belief that children are able to consent to sex in the same way that adults can, and that children enjoy sex. This schema can also allow those who think this way to believe that it is okay for adults to "teach" children about sex by initiating the children's first sexual experiences. Because of their schema, these people may tell themselves that it is okay to have sex with children because they believe they are "teaching" the children a "caring" way, and are maybe even serving as "mentors" to those children.

- **Entitlement** ("I can do whatever I want"). According to this schema, one believes it is okay to have sex with whomever a person wants, and that everyone deserves to have sex. The schema can also include the belief that because someone feels sexually aroused or interested, it is okay to go out and find someone else to have sex with, even if that other person does not want to have sex.

- **Dangerous World** ("The world is a dangerous place"). Someone with this schema believes the world is a violent and uncontrollable place. The belief often includes the schema that others are "out to get you" and that it is okay to gain benefits and satisfaction in any way one can. This belief is often—but not always—based on a person's past experiences.

- **Personality and Sexuality Are Uncontrollable**. According to this schema people were born a certain way or became a certain way and they are not going to change, so even attempting to change is pointless. In this schema, the same principles apply to sexuality: "This is who I am." The person who holds this schema often views committing sexual abuse as behavior that is outside of his control. He believes it is okay to act on his sexual desires, even if the other person doesn't or can't consent to sex.

- **Sexual Activity Without Other Violence Is Not Harmful**. This schema is the belief that sexual behavior is only abusive when it involves clear acts of intentional physical violence. This schema leads people to commit sexual abuse that is still harmful, but just in ways other than through violence. People with this schema often do not recognize the other types of harm that sexual abuse causes, such as psychological harm.

Exercise 3.1: My Schemas

Now that you've had an introduction to schemas, think about how schemas have played a role in your life. The goal of the questions below is to allow you to begin to understand how your beliefs affect your behavior.

1. What are some schemas you have used in your life so far?

2. How do your own schemas affect your interpretations of situations, events, and other people?

3. How do your own schemas affect your reactions to situations, events, and other people?

4. Think about the "mental shortcuts" you have used during your life. Which of the specific schemas or shortcuts above do you think you might have used? Please explain.

5. What other kinds of schemas do you think might have been involved in your sexual offending?

6. What schemas do you think might have been involved in your other offending?

Exercise 3.2: My Reactions to Situations

Let's look at some other ways people react to situations in their daily lives. Having read about all the factors that can affect people's responses to situations, consider the following examples in the ways these situations might apply to you. The goal of this exercise is to start to understand how you respond—your schemas, emotions, thinking, perceptions, beliefs, and behaviors. This is all part of your own self-regulation, which you will look at in more detail later. Consider each situation or example below and answer honestly how you would react in each situation.

Situation 1: You are driving home and someone cuts you off, nearly causing you to have an accident.

1. My first thoughts would be:

   ____

   ____

   ____

2. My emotions would be:

   ____

   ____

   ____

3. What I would do:

   ____

   ____

   ____

Situation 2: You are driving home and someone cuts you off, nearly causing you to have an accident. As you look at the person, you see that he is an elderly man who seems to be having trouble seeing because it is dark.

1. My first thoughts would be:

   ____

   ____

   ____

2. My emotions would be:

3. What I would do:

Situation 3: You are driving home and someone cuts you off, nearly causing you to have an accident. As you look at the person, you see it is a guy from work who doesn't like you and who is always causing problems for you.

1. My first thoughts would be:

2. My emotions would be:

3. What I would do:

4. Now, look back at your answers to all three situations. What is the same about your answers? What is different about your answers? Thinking about your own experiences, attitudes, and beliefs, why would you have responded differently to each of these different situations? What schemas would have affected your reaction to each situation?

Situation 4: You are making a delivery to an office as a part of your job. The receptionist smiles at you. She is very attractive.

1. My first thoughts would be:

2. My emotions would be:

3. What I believe she would be thinking:

4. What I believe she would be feeling:

5. What I would do:

Situation 5: You are making a delivery to an office as a part of your job. The receptionist smiles at you. She is very attractive. She has pictures of herself with a man and two children on display on her desk.

1. My first thoughts would be:

2. My emotions would be:

3. What I believe she would be thinking:

4. What I believe she would be feeling:

5. What I would do:

Situation 6: You are making a delivery to an office as a part of your job. The receptionist smiles at you. She is very attractive. She has pictures of herself with a man and two children on display on her desk. She sees you looking at them and describes how she lost them in a car accident several months ago. Tears start to fill her eyes.

1. My first thoughts would be:

   ____

   ____

   ____

2. My emotions would be:

   ____

   ____

   ____

3. What I believe she would be thinking:

   ____

   ____

   ____

4. What I believe she would be feeling:

   ____

   ____

   ____

5. What I would do:

   ____

   ____

   ____

6. Now, look back at your answers to these situations. What is the same about your answers? What is different about your answers? Thinking about your own experiences, attitudes, and beliefs, why would you have responded differently to each of these different situations? What schemas would have affected your reaction to each situation?

Situation 7: You are in a bar near a pool table. A man with a pool stick whom you don't recognize comes toward you.

1. My first thoughts would be:

2. My emotions would be:

3. What I believe he would be thinking:

4. What I believe he would be feeling:

____

____

____

5. What I would do:

____

____

____

Situation 8: You are in a bar near a pool table. A man with a pool stick whom you don't recognize comes toward you. He asks who you're looking at.

1. My first thoughts would be:

____

____

____

2. My emotions would be:

____

____

____

3. What I believe he would be thinking:

____

____

____

4. What I believe he would be feeling:

____

____

____

5. What I would do:

____

____

____

Situation 9: You are in a bar near a pool table. A man with a pool stick comes toward you. He asks who you're looking at. He then begins to smile, laughs, grabs your shoulder, and asks why you don't remember him from high school. He accurately tells you the name of the teacher whose class you were both in.

1. My first thoughts would be:

____

____

____

2. My emotions would be:

____

____

____

3. What I believe he would be thinking:

____

____

____

4. What I believe he would be feeling:

____

____

____

5. What I would do:

____

____

____

6. Now, look back at your answers to all three situations. What is the same about your answers? What is different about your answers? Thinking about your own experiences, attitudes, and beliefs, why would you have responded differently to each of these different situations? What schemas would have affected your reaction to each situation?

Situation 10: Your neighbor's daughter, an attractive 13-year-old girl, tells you she has trouble meeting mature friends and that no one understands her.

1. My first thoughts would be:

2. My emotions would be:

3. What I believe she would be thinking:

4. What I believe she would be feeling:

5. What I would do:

Situation 11: Your neighbor's daughter, an attractive 13-year-old girl, tells you she has trouble meeting mature friends and that no one understands her. She tells you she used to have a boyfriend, but she doesn't anymore.

1. My first thoughts would be:

2. My emotions would be:

3. What I believe she would be thinking:

4. What I believe she would be feeling:

___

___

___

5. What I would do:

___

___

___

Situation 12: Your neighbor's daughter, an attractive 13-year-old girl, tells you she has trouble meeting mature friends and that no one understands her. She tells you she used to have a boyfriend, but that she doesn't anymore. She then talks about how someone your age once tried to molest her, that she didn't like it, and that the man who did that is now in trouble with the police.

1. My first thoughts would be:

___

___

___

2. My emotions would be:

___

___

___

3. What I believe she would be thinking:

___

___

___

4. What I believe she would be feeling:

___

___

___

5. What I would do:

6. Now, look back at your answers to all three situations. What is the same about your answers? What is different about your answers? Thinking about your own experiences, attitudes, and beliefs, why would you have responded differently to each of these different situations? What schemas would have affected your reaction to each situation?

Situation 13: A woman walks up to you at a dance and seems to flirt with you. She tells you that you had better watch out; it's a crazy world out there. You don't understand what she means, but you think she's attracted to you.

1. My first thoughts would be:

2. My emotions would be:

___

___

___

3. What I believe she would be thinking:

___

___

___

4. What I believe she would be feeling:

___

___

___

5. What I would do:

___

___

___

Situation 14: A woman walks up to you at a dance and seems to flirt with you. You can't quite hear what she's saying but she tells you that you had better watch out; it's a crazy world out there. You don't understand what she means, but you think she's attracted to you. You flirt back with her, and she walks away smiling.

1. My first thoughts would be:

___

___

___

2. My emotions would be:

___

___

___

3. What I believe she would be thinking:

4. What I believe she would be feeling:

5. What I would do:

Situation 15: A woman walks up to you at a dance and seems to flirt with you. You can't quite hear what she's saying but she tells you that you had better watch out; it's a crazy world out there. You don't understand what she means, but you think she's attracted to you. You flirt back with her and she walks away smiling over her shoulder at you. She comes back with a man who angrily tells you that you misunderstood her. She was trying to tell you that there have been some guys acting crazy in the parking lot and to be careful going home.

1. My first thoughts would be:

2. My emotions would be:

3. What I believe she would be thinking:

4. What I believe she would be feeling:

5. What I would do:

6. Now, look back at your answers to these situations. What is the same about your answers? What is different about your answers? Thinking about your own experiences, attitudes, and beliefs, why would you have responded differently to each of these different situations? What schemas would have affected your reaction to each situation?

Clearly, each of these examples is designed to reflect several possible situations. Not every situation means what a person thinks it does. Sometimes the person simply doesn't have enough information to judge a situation, even though he might think he does. But regardless of not having enough information, the person will rely on the "mental shortcuts"—schemas—to interpret the situation in order to decide how to respond.

7. How did having additional information change your response to the situations described above? What assumptions did you make when you didn't have a lot of information? What schemas did you use to "fill in the blanks" when you didn't have all of the information?

____

____

____

____

____

____

____

____

____

____

Exercise 3.3: My Reaction Patterns

Now, look over your answers again to the situations in exercise 3.2 and the differences and similarities you noted. Think deeply about the ways you view yourself, other people, and the world in general. The idea here is to look for patterns in your thinking, emotions, behaviors, beliefs, attitudes, and schemas. For each of the statements below, based on these patterns, circle a number from 0 to 10 indicating how characteristic this is of you—0 is "not at all like me" and 10 is "very much like me."

1. I tend to react to situations impulsively or without thinking:

0	1	2	3	4	5	6	7	8	9	10
Not at all like me					Somewhat like me					Very much like me

2. I tend more to plan what I do and how I react or respond:

0	1	2	3	4	5	6	7	8	9	10
Not at all like me					Somewhat like me					Very much like me

3. I tend to react to situations angrily:

0	1	2	3	4	5	6	7	8	9	10
Not at all like me					Somewhat like me					Very much like me

4. I just don't seem to have what it takes to stay out of trouble:

0	1	2	3	4	5	6	7	8	9	10
Not at all like me					Somewhat like me					Very much like me

5. I tend to be suspicious of other people's motives:

0	1	2	3	4	5	6	7	8	9	10
Not at all like me					Somewhat like me					Very much like me

6. I tend to react or respond without thinking about the other person or his or her motives:

0	1	2	3	4	5	6	7	8	9	10
Not at all like me					Somewhat like me					Very much like me

7. I don't feel much empathy for people I don't like:

0	1	2	3	4	5	6	7	8	9	10
Not at all like me					Somewhat like me					Very much like me

8. I find it difficult to consider another person's point of view before I respond:

0	1	2	3	4	5	6	7	8	9	10
Not at all like me					Somewhat like me					Very much like me

9. I believe that most people generally cannot be trusted:

0	1	2	3	4	5	6	7	8	9	10
Not at all like me					Somewhat like me					Very much like me

10. I believe that it is better to "get" someone before that person "gets" me first:

0	1	2	3	4	5	6	7	8	9	10
Not at all like me					Somewhat like me					Very much like me

11. I believe that having sex can be good for some children:

0	1	2	3	4	5	6	7	8	9	10
Not at all like me					Somewhat like me					Very much like me

12. I believe that it is okay to fight back if a person disrespects me:

0	1	2	3	4	5	6	7	8	9	10
Not at all like me					Somewhat like me					Very much like me

13. I am a very sexual person and need to have sex when I want it:

0	1	2	3	4	5	6	7	8	9	10
Not at all like me					Somewhat like me					Very much like me

Self-Regulation

Now that you have looked at part of self-regulation—your schemas and the patterns in your reactions—this next section will focus more specifically on self-regulation with respect to meeting your goals.

Self-Regulation and Goals

Part of self-regulation refers to how people go about meeting or trying to meet their goals. This involves *planning*, *decision making*, *evaluating what happens*, and *changing* one's behavior as needed. People are *goal-directed*—they work toward meeting their goals and toward getting what they want in life, in both the short term and over the longer term. In chapter 2 of this book, you explored some of the long-term goals you have in your life. Of course, some people focus more on their short-term goals than their long-term goals, and vice versa. It can be especially easy to forget one's long-term goals in the heat of the moment when you are *reacting* quickly to events without giving the events much thought. This reaction is in contrast to the times you slow down, consider the situation, and then decide how best to *respond* to an event in a way that is in line with your long-term goals. Lastly, sometimes the various ways people go about meeting their goals can cause serious problems for themselves or for others, and additionally can result in harm being done to others.

It can be useful to think about goals as being future achievements you wish to either *approach* or *avoid*. For example, setting a goal of getting a job is an *approach goal*. The job is something you want and something you are working toward getting. By contrast, setting a goal of not getting into any more trouble is an *avoidance goal*. Trouble is something you hope will not happen and something you want to prevent or avoid. Research shows that people who organize their lives around approach goals—that are *positive goals*—tend to be happier and less distressed than people who focus on avoidance goals. For this reason, it is worthwhile to think very carefully about the goals you have in life. We will return to these themes later in the workbook.

Approach and avoidance goals are often two sides of the same issue. It is easier to accomplish an approach goal of keeping calm at all times than it is to have an avoidance goal of not letting things irritate or bother you. The common life goals you explored in chapter 2 were designed to be long-term, positive approach goals. In this part of the workbook, you will look at *negative approach goals*, the ones that are related to offending. You will also look at your own self-regulation in general and as it might have played a role in your offenses. First, it is important to examine three different overall styles of self-regulation.

Self-Regulation Styles

In the previous sections and in the exercises you have just completed, you have looked at your patterns of reactions and your responses to a variety of situations. In your treatment work, you also have learned that people manage their behavior and reactions in three basic ways. These are as follows:

Under-Regulation

Under-regulation happens when you do not know what to do in a situation and so you do nothing, or you try to ignore what is happening. You simply may not have the skills to deal with the situation.

Example #1: You have a problem but don't do anything to solve it, hoping the problem will just go away. In this case, even though you might want to work on the problem, you don't know what to do or how to solve the problem, and so you are stuck.

Example #2: You feel inappropriate sexual urges or desires (such as desiring to have sex with a child or wishing to perform acts of sexual aggression against someone), and you try not to think about those urges and desires. In this instance, you want to avoid acting on your urges, but you don't know what to do with those desires, so you don't do anything other than try to ignore them.

Donnie grew up in the system. He was in 10 foster homes and two residential programs after he sexually abused his stepsister. Donnie didn't get much out of treatment, and didn't really see the point of it. As he grew up and became a parent, Donnie knew he shouldn't force himself on his daughter, and he usually tried to ignore his urges to have sex with her. Although this strategy seemed to work for him sometimes, whenever he felt depressed and didn't care about anything, he seemed to "fall apart," and then he forced his daughter to have sex. As he got older, he mostly managed his life by trying to ignore his problems and waiting for them to go away or waiting for someone else to solve them. Donnie felt as though life was passing him by, but he felt powerless to do much about it. Whenever he felt like he wasn't living up to his potential, he would try to avoid those thoughts, as well.

Donnie had urges to have sex with his daughter, but he hadn't tried to stop those urges. He didn't work on controlling his urges during treatment, either, and he didn't work on strategies to control his sexual desires. Donnie also did not have or use any problem-solving skills to deal with his life problems. As a result, he often felt powerless. Because he did nothing about his issues, he would feel bad sometimes, but all he did was try to avoid thinking about how he felt. Donnie's self-regulation style is *under-regulation*. Donnie put himself at risk because when things got especially bad, he gave up trying, he felt like he was out of control, and he offended against his daughter.

Mis-Regulation

Mis-regulation happens when you see that a problem exists and try to do something about it. Your strategies, however, do not resolve the situation and, in fact, may often make it worse.

Example #1: You feel depressed or angry and drink or use drugs to feel better. In this case, drinking or doing drugs may make you feel better over the short term, but that strategy does not solve your depression or anger problems over the long term. Drinking also causes you to be even more depressed, and may also remove your inhibitions against acting on your anger, so you actually become more aggressive.

Example #2: You have inappropriate sexual fantasies and masturbate to them so as not to act out physically against someone. Over the long term, however, this behavior actually strengthens the relationship between inappropriate fantasies and the willingness to act on them. Masturbating to inappropriate fantasies actually makes it more likely you will act out those fantasies on others.

As a child, Chris never had the opportunities that many of his friends had. His father left the family when Chris was still young, and Chris blamed himself. Because of a number of problems he had as he grew up, Chris attended lots of treatment programs. He was never entirely happy, however, and he had little ambition for himself other than working in the local businesses in his small town. He struggled with depression and anxiety, and he always felt he never quite had the skills he needed to "make it" in life. Chris had great ideas about how to solve problems and face challenges, but his ideas never seemed to work very well. Chris discovered he had a sexual interest in children. Whenever he was close to a child, he would try to think of skills he could use so that he wouldn't abuse the child. His efforts to deal with his sexual feelings about children led to masturbating a lot in the hope that he would become less aroused when he saw a child. Chris looked at pornography involving teenagers almost every night. He told himself that at least he wasn't touching a child. Unfortunately, the pornography didn't help Chris, and, in fact, he found that his sexual urges toward children increased. Chris told himself, "I've tried everything I can do to not approach those kids. Maybe being drawn to children is just who I am. Nothing else seems to work for me."

Through his use of pornography, Chris was trying to manage and lessen his sexual interest in children. Yet instead of using skills that might have worked to reduce the attraction and arousal he felt toward children, Chris masturbated to pornography. Although his use of pornography meant that Chris did try to use a skill, it wasn't a strategy that was effective. In fact, trying to cope by masturbating just made things worse for Chris until, finally, he gave up trying to control himself and began abusing children. Chris's self-regulation style is mis-regulation.

Controlled Self-Regulation

Controlled self-regulation is when you are able to control your reactions in a situation, but you still harm someone or create problems because harming another person is actually your goal or because you want to meet your goals regardless of what the other person wants.

Example #1: You follow a potential victim and watch until that person is alone so you can then approach the person when the opportunity arises. Those situations might occur such as when the other person is alone or when no one else is around to see or catch you. In this example, you are able to control yourself, but you do so in a way that causes harm to others.

Example #2: You place yourself in situations where sexually abusing people might become a possibility. For example, you might take a job at a nightclub and wait around until the end of the evening, when people are more likely to be intoxicated. You are not deliberately seeking out specific victims, but you are ready and able to cause harm when the opportunity arises. In every sense, you are able to control your behavior. The difference is that you are willing to engage in crimes.

> *Terry grew up in a home where he learned from his father that women are basically either bitches or whores—they say "yes" when they mean "no," and "no" when they mean "yes." Either way, Terry was convinced it was impossible to ever really get close to women. For that matter, he believed no one in the world was really trustworthy, women especially. In school, Terry got good grades, but he always dreamed of joining an outlaw motorcycle gang. He never felt as though he got along with "ordinary" people, and he tended to be suspicious of other people's motives. Just the same, he was usually able to accomplish just about anything he set out to do. One day, Terry decided he wanted to have sex with a woman he had seen on his street. He began to think of ways he could assault her when no one was looking. He was very interested in having sex, but only under situations that he could control and only when he would not be caught by anyone.*

In this example, Terry is very much in control, and so his self-regulation style is *controlled self-regulation.* Terry does not have a problem controlling his behavior; the problem he has is that he uses his skills to harm people and to sexually assault women.

Self-regulation is a very important aspect of offending (both sexual offending as well as other types of offending). Self-regulation is involved in all life problems, and also plays a role in meeting goals in life. Because self-regulation is so important to many aspects of life, it is important that you discover what style of self-regulation you tend to use. Although self-regulation can sometimes be different depending on the situation, you should be able to discover and understand your own overall style. The questions in the next exercise will help you to understand your self-regulation style and the ways you manage yourself.

Exercise 3.4: My Self-Regulation Style

This exercise provides an opportunity to explore how you have self-regulated your responses to situations in the past.

1. How do you usually feel when you are experiencing stress?

2. What do you usually do to cope with stress? Do these strategies work? Why or why not?

3. What do you usually do to manage your emotions? Do these strategies work? Why or why not?

4. How do you usually deal with problems that you experience? Do these strategies work? Why or why not?

5. Do you sometimes feel overwhelmed in certain situations? Which ones? What do you do when you find yourself in those situations?

6. How often do you act without thinking, or, in other words, do things impulsively? What happens?

7. If you desperately want something, are you able to wait or do you feel like you need to have it *right away*? What do you do in those situations?

8. Do you ever feel that you are not in control of your thoughts, emotions, or behavior? In what situations do you feel this way? What do you do when you feel you are not in control?

9. What skills or strategies do you use to control your behavior, when you have to?

10. Did you feel overwhelmed or out of control during your most recent sexual offense? What happened? What did you do when you felt overwhelmed?

____

____

____

____

____

____

____

____

11. Have you felt overwhelmed or out of control during other offenses (sexual or other crimes)? What happened? What did you do?

____

____

____

____

____

____

____

____

12. How do you usually deal with your sexual urges?

____

____

____

____

13. How do you usually deal with your anger or your feelings of aggression?

14. How did you deal with your sexual urges during your most recent sexual offense? What about during other offenses (sexual or other types)?

15. During your offenses, did you feel like you could control your sexual arousal or urges? Why or why not? How much in control of your actions would you say you were during your offenses? Were there times when you felt more in control and times when you felt less in control? What happened in each instance? What were some of the differences between when you felt more in control and less in control?

____

____

____

____

____

____

____

____

16. What kinds of things might you have done to prevent your most recent sexual offense from happening?

____

____

____

____

____

____

____

____

17. If you encountered a similar situation in the future, what level of control over your urges do you think you would have?

____

____

____

18. What kinds of things might you have done to prevent your other offenses from happening (sexual or other crimes)?

19. If you knew someone who was about to offend sexually, what would you tell him about how he could prevent committing the offense?

20. Having read this part of the workbook, and having answered the previous questions, check the self-regulation type you believe best matches you.

    - ❒ Under-regulation
    - ❒ Mis-regulation
    - ❒ Controlled regulation

21. Why did you choose this style?

22. Are there times when you react with a different style depending on the situation? For example, some people may have controlled regulation at their jobs, but under-regulation in their intimate relationships. How does your self-regulation change depending on the type of situation?

Summary

In this part of the workbook, you have explored how people react to situations based on a number of different factors. These factors are shaped by people's cognitive schemas, which are the mental shortcuts that people take to make sense of situations quickly. Cognitive schemas are shaped by people's interpretations of situations, their attitudes toward other people, their own personal experiences, and other factors. You've also explored self-regulation styles and have examined how these styles fit into your life. This assessment will be important later in this workbook, where you will come to a better understanding of how schemas and self-regulation styles fit into your offense chain and how they will help shape your good life plan for the future. This understanding will also be important in your overall treatment, since factors such as schemas and self-regulation have a strong influence on people's lives. Also, sometimes schemas and self-regulation can be risk factors for re-offending or can be linked to risk factors.

The next part of this workbook focuses on risk factors. In that section, you will discover risk factors that can make it more likely for you to re-offend. Learning about these risk factors will help you know where you may need to make changes in order to prevent re-offending, with the goal of having a good life that does not involve offending.

CHAPTER 4

Understanding My Risk Factors

In the last section, you looked at your thinking patterns and your self-regulation, both of which are related to offending and to various life problems. In this section, you will look in more detail at specific factors that cause you to be at risk to commit a sexual offense. A *risk factor* is anything that makes a sexual offense or re-offense likely to happen. Risk factors exist not only for sexual crimes but also for violent and other types of crimes. Sometimes risk factors are the same for different types of offenses, and sometimes there are different factors for different types of offenses. Researchers have identified certain specific risk factors, which are described later in this chapter.

In this section of the workbook, you will look at your own personal risk factors, so you can better understand what might lead you to re-offend. Having a better understanding of those risk factors will help you to develop specific skills and strategies in treatment so you can reduce your risk and develop a satisfying good life plan for yourself.

Even though you may be highly motivated to prevent offending again, it is important to remember that because you offended in the past, you have the potential to offend again in the future. For that reason, it is essential to learn about and manage your risk factors. Unfortunately, even the best commitment and motivation aren't enough to prevent re-offending.

Remember from previous parts of this workbook that, over time and throughout their lives, all people develop patterns that cause them to respond in certain ways. When it comes to offending, these patterns can lead to crimes and can become strong patterns of behavior. For example, certain things about you and your life made it likely that you would commit a sexual offense or another crime. This section is about looking in detail at some of those patterns and factors, helping you to find ways to manage your risk so you don't offend again. As you will also learn, sometimes your life goals have not been met because of some of the same risk factors that are related to your offending.

No single factor causes a person to commit sexual harm. Most often, it is a *combination* of factors that leads to sexual harm. For example, a person might have a sexual attraction to children, but be unwilling to act on that interest. In this case, it would require two risk factors—sexual attraction to children and being willing to have sex with them—for a sex offense to happen. So it is important to know both your risk factors as well as the exact combination of these factors that can lead to offending. It is also important to note that the ways these risk factors can influence behavior is different from one person to the next. For one person, the combination of sexual attraction toward children and a willingness to act on that attraction may be necessary for him to offend. For another person, a sexual preference for children might be all he needs to pursue a child sexually, simply because he wants to have an intimate or sexual encounter and a child is available.

One particularly challenging thing about understanding risk factors is that they can be much easier to manage in some circumstances than in others. For example, some people have an easier time managing their sexual urges when they are not also experiencing stress. Others can manage their behavior when they stay away from drugs or alcohol. It can be helpful to think of some risk factors as existing within you, and others as existing outside you in your environment.

Types of Risk Factors

Researchers have learned a lot about risk factors, and that information helps to explain why sexual abuse occurs. As you proceed in this section of the workbook, you will be asked to remember several important things about risk factors.

Some risk factors can be changed by people's actions, and others cannot.

Some risk factors are referred to as *static*, meaning that they cannot be changed by deliberate actions. Examples of static risk factors include your history of offending and your age. You have no control over changing static factors such as these.

By contrast, other risk factors are *dynamic,* meaning that they can change, such as through treatment. Because you can do something about these risk factors, these are the ones that you will be working on in treatment.

Different risk factors are related to different types of offenses, although some risk factors are the same for different types of crimes.

Depending upon your own personal history, you may be more at risk to commit a new sexual offense than to commit another type of crime. By contrast, you may be more at risk to commit a non-sexual violent offense than you are to commit another type of offense, such as a robbery. It is important, however, to look at risk factors across all possibilities in order to manage your risk successfully and to meet your goals in your good life plan.

Some risk factors or combinations of factors are more strongly related to sexual offending than are others.

Researchers have found that certain risk factors have a very strong influence on offending, and have found that some combinations create a *very* high risk. For example, illegal and unusual sexual interests are a very strong risk factor for sexual offending. The combination of this with beliefs or schemas that make a person believe it is okay to offend can be especially linked to re-offending.

Your risk factors are unique to you.

Although certain risk factors have been identified by researchers, your own risk factors and the ways they are combined will be unique to you. At this point, you may already have had a *risk assessment* conducted. A risk assessment is done to help therapists as well as probation and parole officers understand what factors are unique to you so when all of you work together, you and your team can develop specific plans and skills for managing your individual risk factors.

Because your risk factors are unique to you, your therapist may talk about different risk factors than the ones discussed in this workbook. The point is to understand all the possible risk factors and to be able to apply them to yourself so you can then better understand and make the important changes you need to make.

The list below focuses on the risk factors you can change, the ones that are called *dynamic risk factors.* Remember, this list does not include every risk factor, and you may have other risk factors that are not included here. In this section, you will also find questions that can help you decide how much each factor applies to you.

Previous Criminal Behavior/Antisocial Lifestyle

People who have committed crimes for a long time often have a hard time stopping their criminal behavior, because doing something over and over again can turn behaviors into habits. Committing crime is no different from any other habit. In addition to becoming a habit, people often develop cognitive schemas that support committing crimes. Such schemas can include attitudes and justifications like, "Being a criminal is who I am," or "Committing crimes is what I know best." Habit, schemas, and opportunities to offend, alone or in combination, make it more likely a person will continue offending. Previous criminal behavior or an antisocial lifestyle may simply indicate that the person finds committing crimes acceptable and sees no reason to change. Previous criminal behavior and an antisocial lifestyle are risk factors for both sexual and other crimes.

1. How much does your past criminal behavior play a role in your daily life?

0	1	2	3	4	5	6	7	8	9	10
Not at all					Somewhat					A lot

2. How much has your past criminal behavior played a role in non-sexual crimes you have committed?

0	1	2	3	4	5	6	7	8	9	10
Not at all					Somewhat					A lot

3. How much has your past criminal behavior played a role in sexual crimes you have committed?

0	1	2	3	4	5	6	7	8	9	10
Not at all					Somewhat					A lot

4. How much has your past criminal behavior interfered with meeting your life goals?

0	1	2	3	4	5	6	7	8	9	10
Not at all					Somewhat					A lot

5. Provide below a short description of some of the ways your past criminal behavior plays a role in your offending and creates problems meeting your life goals. Please be specific.

____

____

____

____

____

Illegal or Unusual Sexual Interests

This category refers to being interested in, or even preferring, sexual activity or objects that are outside what is normal for most people. Not all of these interests are illegal, but they can cause problems nonetheless. Having problematic sexual interests is a very strong risk factor for sexual offending and re-offending, because these types of sexual interests and preferences are very powerful. Acting on these interests can also be very rewarding to certain people, due to the short-term positive feelings that often come with sexual activity. A sexual preference for illegal activities, such as sexual aggression, combined with a belief that one is entitled to act on these interests, can especially lead to offending. Three types of risk factors present in this area are:

Sexual Interest in Children. This term refers to an adult who is sexually interested in children. It also refers to a person who would prefer to have sex and/or be intimate with a child than with an adult. People who have a sexual preference for children would rather, if given the choice, have their intimate or sexual relationships be with children. They may have relationships with adults, but they would prefer to have their sexual relationships with children. Others have relationships with both adults and children, being interested in sexual activity with children without a preference. Regardless, people with an interest or preference also often hold attitudes and beliefs that make it seem acceptable to have sex with children, despite society's laws. They believe that children are interested in, or knowledgeable about, sex in the same ways that adults are. They may feel they relate better to children than to adults or may feel more comfortable in the company of children than adults, think that children are truly capable of consenting to sex, or believe that children actively desire sex or that they are okay with it. All of these beliefs make it likely a person will pursue sexual behavior with children.

1. How much does sexual interest in children play a role in your daily life? That is, how much are you interested in or would you prefer to have sexual or intimate relationships with children?

0	1	2	3	4	5	6	7	8	9	10
Not at all					Somewhat					A lot

2. How much has sexual interest in children played a role in your non-sexual offending?

0	1	2	3	4	5	6	7	8	9	10
Not at all					Somewhat					A lot

3. How much has sexual interest in children played a role in your sexual offending?

0	1	2	3	4	5	6	7	8	9	10
Not at all					Somewhat					A lot

4. Provide below a short description of some of the ways sexual interest in children plays a role in your offending or creates problems meeting your goals. Please be specific.

____

____

____

____

____

Sexual Interest in Coercion or Rape. Some people enjoy the forceful aspects of sexual assault as much or more than the sex itself. People who have a sexual preference for coercion or rape would rather, if given the choice, have sexual relationships that involve coercion or force than consensual sex. For example, a person may rape someone because he gets the sense of power and control that he wants in a relationship. When people have these preferences, they are at risk because they are not able to have consensual sex. They may also enjoy the other person's suffering, humiliation, or fear. Sometimes they may have an interest but not a preference, but this is a risk factor as well.

1. How much does sexual interest in coercion or rape play a role in your daily life? That is, how much are you interested in or would even prefer to have coerced or forced sex in your relationships?

0	1	2	3	4	5	6	7	8	9	10
Not at all					Somewhat					A lot

2. How much has sexual interest in coercion or rape played a role in your non-sexual offending?

0	1	2	3	4	5	6	7	8	9	10
Not at all					Somewhat					A lot

3. How much has sexual interest in coercion or rape played a role in your sexual offending?

0	1	2	3	4	5	6	7	8	9	10
Not at all					Somewhat					A lot

4. Provide below a short description of some of the ways sexual interest in coercion or rape plays a role in your offending or creates problems meeting your goals. Please be specific.

____

____

____

____

____

Multiple Interests or Preferences. Sometimes people have more than one sexual interest or preference. This combination can be especially problematic. For example, a person might have a sexual interest in stealing women's underwear as well as a sexual interest in raping women. Having more than one interest or preference makes it more likely that a person will offend or re-offend. For some people, it can be the case that the more sexual interests a person has, the more they create opportunities to act on those interests.

1. How much do multiple interests or preferences play a role in your daily life?

0	1	2	3	4	5	6	7	8	9	10
Not at all					Somewhat					A lot

2. How much have multiple interests or preferences played a role in your non-sexual offending?

0	1	2	3	4	5	6	7	8	9	10
Not at all					Somewhat					A lot

3. How much have multiple interests or preferences played a role in your sexual offending?

0	1	2	3	4	5	6	7	8	9	10
Not at all					Somewhat					A lot

4. Provide below a short description of some of the ways multiple interests or preferences play a role in your offending or create problems meeting your goals. Please be specific.

____

____

____

____

____

General Self-Regulation

When looking at risk factors, different types of self-regulation play a role. The first risk factor is known as *general self-regulation* or *overall self-regulation*. This risk factor refers to your ability to manage your thoughts, emotions, and behavior in day-to-day life and in offending. When you have problems with general self-regulation, you are also likely to have problems meeting your life goals. Problems with general self-regulation create risk factors for all types of crimes. General self-regulation is made up of four separate risk factors: *impulsivity, difficulties with solving problems, negative emotionality,* and *resistance to rules.* Each of these is described below.

Impulsivity. This term means doing things without thinking or acting on the "spur of the moment." People who are impulsive react without thinking about the consequences of their actions. Sometimes they have low levels of self-control. They often talk about things happening so quickly that, when they are asked about it, they say they didn't know what happened in the situation. Examples of impulsivity can include not following through on commitments or plans, quitting a job without having another one to go to, getting into fights, and doing risky things without planning ahead and without considering the consequences.

1. How much does impulsivity play a role in your daily life?

0	1	2	3	4	5	6	7	8	9	10
Not at all					Somewhat					A lot

2. How much has impulsivity played a role in your non-sexual offending?

0	1	2	3	4	5	6	7	8	9	10
Not at all					Somewhat					A lot

3. How much has impulsivity played a role in your sexual offending?

0	1	2	3	4	5	6	7	8	9	10
Not at all					Somewhat					A lot

4. Provide below a short description of some of the ways impulsivity plays a role in your offending or creates problems meeting your goals. Please be specific.

____

____

____

____

____

Difficulties with Solving Problems. Problem-solving is a complex skill that involves the steps people take to solve problems they are experiencing. Problem-solving skills require that a person understands exactly what the problem is and then comes up with ways to solve it. Next, he needs to go back to the situation and evaluate how well his solution worked. Through that process, he can learn better how to solve the next problem he faces.

When people have difficulty solving problems, that difficulty can lead to offending as well as not being able to meet life goals. Such problems happen when people don't assess situations correctly, don't choose the right solution to a problem, or don't look at their responses afterward to learn from the situation how to solve the problem better the next time. For example, a person who is unable to find work may not have the skills to define the problem properly. In this case, the person needs to figure out whether his inability to find a job has to do with his lack of education, his lack of skills for job interviews, or his lack of motivation. When a person can't define what the problem is, he cannot come up with ways to solve it: he won't know whether to go back to school, adjust his attitude, or get training on how to succeed at job interviews. Meeting life goals also involves solving problems along the way. For example, one needs to be able to figure out how to behave most effectively in a lot of different situations in order to have a sense of personal choice. Problem-solving skills are crucial for negotiating situations effectively, such as at work and in relationships. Sometimes, a person needs to be able to solve problems quickly. Being unable to solve problems and acquire the strength of personal choice and independence places someone at risk to seek empowerment in ways that harm others. Fortunately, learning and practicing simple problem-solving skills can help prevent further crimes.

1. How much do difficulties solving problems play a role in your daily life?

0	1	2	3	4	5	6	7	8	9	10
Not at all					Somewhat					A lot

2. How much have difficulties solving problems played a role in your non-sexual offending?

0	1	2	3	4	5	6	7	8	9	10
Not at all					Somewhat					A lot

3. How much do difficulties solving problems play a role in your sexual offending?

0	1	2	3	4	5	6	7	8	9	10
Not at all					Somewhat					A lot

4. Provide below a short description of some of the ways that difficulties solving problems play a role in your offending or create problems meeting your goals. Please be specific.

____

____

____

____

____

Negative Emotionality. This term refers to chronically feeling hostile toward others, being angry all the time, or having the belief that others are out to cause you problems. If you have negative emotionality, you can believe that the world has done you wrong, that others are responsible for your problems, or that you would like to punish other people for the things that have gone wrong in your life. Negative emotionality often results in having to get respect from others and on getting revenge when you feel disrespected. Sometimes people with negative emotionality are described as "having a chip on their shoulder," meaning that they are always ready for an argument or a fight, or that they tend to always see the negative side of things. For example, one person may constantly feel that others treat him badly, which can lead to feeling revenge against other people and also to getting into lots of fights. When people have negative emotionality, their desire to feel better can lead to offending or harming others whom they believe have done wrong to them.

1. How much does negative emotionality play a role in your daily life?

0	1	2	3	4	5	6	7	8	9	10
Not at all					Somewhat					A lot

2. How much has negative emotionality played a role in your non-sexual offending?

0	1	2	3	4	5	6	7	8	9	10
Not at all					Somewhat					A lot

3. How much has negative emotionality played a role in your sexual offending?

0	1	2	3	4	5	6	7	8	9	10
Not at all					Somewhat					A lot

4. Provide below a short description of some of the ways negative emotionality plays a role in your offending or creates problems meeting your goals. Please be specific.

____

____

____

____

____

Resistance to Rules and Supervision. This is the term used when someone has problems following rules or when someone does not want to follow rules. Sometimes, people don't think certain rules apply to them. Sometimes, they pick and choose the rules they think make sense and disregard the ones that don't. Of course, not following rules leads to problems and to offending, because that's when people can get into trouble or break the law. Resistance to rules and supervision can also include acting out in school, which then can lead to being suspended or expelled. Resistance to rules can also include the ways people defy authority, when they refuse to cooperate with supervision and then violate their release conditions. Resistance can also include having a negative attitude about rules and restrictions that have been set by the court or by law-enforcement personnel or others in positions of authority. This attitude can seriously affect the relationships these people have with those who are trying to help them be crime-free.

1. How much does resistance to rules play a role in your daily life?

0	1	2	3	4	5	6	7	8	9	10
Not at all					Somewhat					A lot

2. How much has resistance to rules and supervision played a role in your non-sexual offending?

0	1	2	3	4	5	6	7	8	9	10
Not at all					Somewhat					A lot

3. How much has resistance to rules and supervision played a role in your sexual offending?

0	1	2	3	4	5	6	7	8	9	10
Not at all					Somewhat					A lot

4. Provide below a short description of some of the ways resistance to rules and supervision plays a role in your offending and creates problems meeting your goals. Please be specific.

____

____

____

____

____

Sexual Self-Regulation

Recall from above that different specific types of self-regulation exist. In the section above, you looked at general or overall self-regulation. Another risk factor in the self-regulation category is specific to sexual behavior. Sexual self-regulation refers to how much a person is able to manage and control his sexual behavior and thoughts. People who have difficulty managing their sexual behavior and thoughts may be impulsive about sex or may feel that they are not able to control their behavior. These people are more likely to act on their problematic sexual urges. It is important to note that this acting out takes many different forms; it does not always mean having sexual intercourse with another person. Instead, sexual self-regulation refers to a variety of activities, including having sex with others, masturbating, thinking about sex, using sex to cope with emotions, and doing activities such as going to strip clubs regularly. Each of these risk factors is described in the text that follows.

Sexual Preoccupation. Being sexually preoccupied has to do with thinking about sex more than most people usually do, or thinking about it so much that it gets in the way of other life goals or causes other problems. For example, sexual preoccupation can result in a person thinking about sex so much that he sometimes has trouble focusing on other things he wants to do. Some people have trouble at work or lose their jobs because they were looking at pornography at work. Sexual preoccupation can also involve frequent and diverse sexual behavior. For example, researchers have found that masturbating six or more times a week can be an indicator of sexual preoccupation among adults. Sexual preoccupation can also take the form of relating sexual meanings to non-sexual situations. This situation happens when people interpret everyday conversations in a sexual way, or when they believe that, because someone is interested in them, this means that person also wants to be sexual with them.

1. How much does sexual preoccupation play a role in your daily life?

0	1	2	3	4	5	6	7	8	9	10
Not at all					Somewhat					A lot

2. How much has sexual preoccupation played a role in your non-sexual offending?

0	1	2	3	4	5	6	7	8	9	10
Not at all					Somewhat					A lot

3. How much has sexual preoccupation played a role in your sexual offending?

0	1	2	3	4	5	6	7	8	9	10
Not at all					Somewhat					A lot

4. Provide below a short description of some of the ways sexual preoccupation plays a role in your offending or creates problems meeting your goals. Please be specific.

____

____

____

____

____

Using Sex to Cope. This risk factor involves using sex as a way to handle emotions and stress. People who follow this pattern use sex as a way to cope with anger or as a way to keep themselves calm or satisfied. While many people have a wide variety of ways to cope with the daily stresses of life, sexual self-regulation problems can occur when sex is one of only a few ways or the main way that someone has to manage his stress and emotions.

1. How much does using sex to cope with stress or emotions play a role in your daily life?

0	1	2	3	4	5	6	7	8	9	10
Not at all					Somewhat					A lot

2. How much has using sex to cope with stress or emotions played a role in your non-sexual offending?

0	1	2	3	4	5	6	7	8	9	10
Not at all					Somewhat					A lot

3. How much has using sex to cope with stress or emotions played a role in your sexual offending?

0	1	2	3	4	5	6	7	8	9	10
Not at all					Somewhat					A lot

4. Provide below a short description of some of the ways you use sex to cope, and describe how this plays a role in your offending or creates problems meeting your goals. Please be specific.

___

___

___

___

___

Schemas, Attitudes, and Beliefs

Your personal schemas can be risk factors for all types of offending. Recall from chapter 3 that people have "filters" or "mental shortcuts" called *cognitive schemas* that guide what the situation means to them, especially when the situation or the best way to respond is unclear.

Many people who cause sexual harm have attitudes and belief systems that make it seem acceptable to them to abuse people or to commit other crimes. People who view criminal behavior as acceptable are more likely to engage in it. Schemas can also take the form of hostility or negative attitudes toward groups of people, such as women, even those they love or care for. This attitude can take the form of believing that women can't be trusted, or that they mean *yes* when they say *no*.

Other schemas lead to beliefs such as, "I have to fight to get even," or "It's a dangerous world, so I have to protect myself and 'get' people before they 'get' me." Such attitudes are based on a person's experiences as well as his beliefs about the world. A person with these schemas is more likely to believe that offending is acceptable behavior. For example, a man with a "dangerous world" schema—who feels that the world has given him a bad deal—may take advantage of an opportunity to harm someone else. From his perspective, harm, revenge, or taking advantage seem like acceptable ways to deal with a world that is dangerous to him.

Different types of schemas can lead to offending, including *crime-supportive schemas* and *abuse-supportive schemas.* Also included here are *cognitive distortions* and an individual's personality.

Crime-Supportive Schemas. These kinds of schemas are risk factors because they allow a person to think that committing crimes is acceptable. These schemas are also risk factors specifically for sexual crimes. Many of these schemas are similar to sexual abuse–related schemas, but many are different, too. You will want to work with your therapist to identify these for you, specifically, but examples of common crime-supportive schemas are such things as, "I want to get things quickly and easily," or "No one is hurt by my behavior."

1. How much do crime-supportive schemas play a role in your daily life?

0	1	2	3	4	5	6	7	8	9	10
Not at all					Somewhat					A lot

2. How much have crime-supportive schemas played a role in your non-sexual offending?

0	1	2	3	4	5	6	7	8	9	10
Not at all					Somewhat					A lot

3. How much have crime-supportive schemas played a role in your sexual offending?

0	1	2	3	4	5	6	7	8	9	10
Not at all					Somewhat					A lot

4. Provide below a short description of some of the ways crime-supportive schemas play a role in your offending or create problems meeting your goals. Please be specific.

____

____

____

____

____

Abuse-Supportive Schemas. These schemas are risk factors because they allow a person to think sexual abuse is acceptable. These schemas can also be risk factors for non-sexual crimes, as well. Abuse-supportive schemas are not the same as the excuses and justifications a person makes after he has committed an offense. Instead, these abuse-supportive schemas include beliefs in one's own sexual entitlement (for example, "I have a right to fulfill my sexual desires," or, "No one has the right to deny me my sexual destiny"). Abuse-supportive schemas also include beliefs that children are able to consent to touching or sex, or that they actually want or seek out sex with adults. Having these beliefs makes it more likely that a person will see sex with children or forced sex as okay.

1. How much do abuse-supportive schemas play a role in your daily life?

0	1	2	3	4	5	6	7	8	9	10
Not at all					Somewhat					A lot

2. How much have abuse-supportive schemas played a role in your non-sexual offending?

0	1	2	3	4	5	6	7	8	9	10
Not at all					Somewhat					A lot

3. How much have abuse-supportive schemas played a role in your sexual offending?

0	1	2	3	4	5	6	7	8	9	10
Not at all					Somewhat					A lot

4. Provide below a short description of some of the ways abuse-supportive schemas play a role in your offending and create problems meeting your goals. Please be specific.

____

____

____

____

____

Cognitive Distortions. As described earlier, cognitive distortions are different from schemas. While schemas are very deeply held beliefs, cognitive distortions are what people tell themselves in a specific situation. Cognitive distortions are the momentary thoughts people have in a specific situation that then allow them to give themselves permission to abuse others or to commit crimes. Cognitive distortions are also the reasons people tell themselves after offending in order to justify or excuse their actions. Cognitive distortions that make sexual offending seem okay include minimizing the abuse, for example, "It was no big deal"; and blaming the victim, for example, "She was asking for it." Other examples include assuming the other person is interested and is consenting to sex when he or she is not, and can include excuses such as, "It's okay for me to do this because I was abused as a child." Examples of cognitive distortions for non-sexual offending include making assumptions about how things will turn out, for example, assuming victims of theft will not be affected by crime because they have insurance. Another example is making assumptions based on limited or innaccurate information, for example, "All my friends break the law, so everyone must do it."

1. How much do cognitive distortions play a role in your daily life?

0	1	2	3	4	5	6	7	8	9	10
Not at all					Somewhat					A lot

2. How much have cognitive distortions played a role in your non-sexual offending?

0	1	2	3	4	5	6	7	8	9	10
Not at all					Somewhat					A lot

3. How much have cognitive distortions played a role in your sexual offending?

0	1	2	3	4	5	6	7	8	9	10
Not at all					Somewhat					A lot

4. Provide below a short description of some of the ways cognitive distortions play a role in your offending or create problems meeting your goals. Please be specific.

____

____

____

____

____

Personality. Some people commit crimes because of personality factors. These factors can include seeing yourself as better than others, having a lack of concern for others, having a tendency to lie or to manipulate others, or having problems understanding the perspective of other people. Often, these aspects of someone's personality work together to make a situation quite risky. For example, if you are the kind of person who sees an opportunity to manipulate someone, who doesn't understand the other person's perspective, or who has no concern for that other person, then you are far more likely to engage in a crime against that person. These risk factors can be extremely difficult for people to see in themselves. Your therapist will have some idea about how your personality fits into your life, although your self-assessment is important, too.

1. How much has your personality played a role in your non-sexual offending?

0	1	2	3	4	5	6	7	8	9	10
Not at all					Somewhat					A lot

2. How much has your personality played a role in your sexual offending?

0	1	2	3	4	5	6	7	8	9	10
Not at all					Somewhat					A lot

3. Provide below a short description of some of the ways your personality plays a role in your offending or creates problems meeting your goals. Please be specific.

____

____

____

____

____

Relationships and Intimacy

Relationships of all kinds play a large role in people's lives. People have many different kinds of relationships—with friends, family, co-workers, intimate partners, neighbors, etc.—and these relationships are important in meeting each person's life goals. But, sometimes problems with relationships can mean that a person cannot meet his goals. Relationship problems can also be part of what causes a person to offend. Relationship problems can be a risk factor for both sexual and non-sexual crimes, because the people we have relationships with influence our behavior, our thoughts, and our attitudes—whether for good or for bad.

For example, consider a person who sees himself as unable to find and maintain healthy friendships with other adults. Now imagine that this person feels as if he is more like a child himself, and therefore feels that only children can really understand him. Now also imagine that the only adults in this person's life with whom he can relate are themselves sexual offenders against children. This person is at obvious risk to believe it is okay to have sex with children and because his friends and associates believe the same. It is therefore likely he would continue to seek out children to have sex with until he makes major changes to his relationships. Three primary risk factors exist in this relationship area: *friends, peers, and associates; a lack of emotionally intimate relationships with adults;* and *emotional connection with children.*

Friends, Peers, and Associates. There is some truth to the saying, "You can tell a lot about a person by the company he keeps." Surrounding yourself with people who commit crimes can keep you at risk for getting into trouble. Even when your friends have been part of your life for many years or even if they are people whom you are hoping to help, unless they themselves are actively seeking to make their own lives better, they can lead you into trouble.

Your friends can have more of an influence on you than you realize. In the case of sexual offending, it can be that others know about your offending but don't do anything about it, leaving you to think that your behavior must not be all that bad or without help when you need it in risky situations. It could also be that your friends talk with you about sex in ways that make it seem okay to abuse. For non-sexual offending, it could be that your friends persuade you to do something illegal. The basic links between your friends and crime have to do with the type and strength of their influence on you. Friends can lead you to crime or lead you away from it.

1. Ask yourself who your friends are: Do they think criminal behavior is okay? How about sexual offending? Are your friends people who feel they've been treated unfairly by the "system"? Do they have pro-crime schemas? Do they help you meet your positive life goals or do they interfere with your life goals?

   ____

   ____

   ____

   ____

   ____

   ____

2. What role do your friends, peers, and associates play in your daily life? For example, are your friends only a little important to you, or are they involved in your life a lot or very important to you?

0	1	2	3	4	5	6	7	8	9	10
Not at all					Somewhat					A lot

3. How much of a role have your friends, peers, or associates played in non-sexual crimes you have committed?

0	1	2	3	4	5	6	7	8	9	10
Not at all					Somewhat					A lot

4. How much have your friends, peers, or associates played a role in sexual crimes you have committed?

0	1	2	3	4	5	6	7	8	9	10
Not at all					Somewhat					A lot

5. How much have your friends or associates created other problems for you?

0	1	2	3	4	5	6	7	8	9	10
Not at all					Somewhat					A lot

6. How much have your friends or associates helped you to meet your life goals?

0	1	2	3	4	5	6	7	8	9	10
Not at all					Somewhat					A lot

7. Provide below a short description of some of the ways your friends, peers, and associates play a role in your offending or cause problems meeting your goals. Please be specific.

____

____

____

____

____

Lack of Intimate Relationships with Adults (also referred to as *intimacy deficits*). This difficulty refers to the times when you have problems developing and keeping stable relationships with other adults. It can include seeing yourself as unable to be in an intimate relationship with an adult partner, seeing yourself as inadequate or unlovable, or having little to no interest in relationships with other adults. This risk factor can also take the form of having low confidence in your own ability to establish close relationships. For example, imagine an adult man who has never been able to form healthy relationships and who believes that adult women are basically "out to get him." Whenever he has tried to get into a relationship, it has seemed to him that the women he has dated have spent most of their time nagging him. He is now in a new relationship with a woman his age, and he thinks that she's either out to take advantage of him or that she is nagging when she doesn't get what she wants. He does not have an understanding of how adult relationships work, and he doesn't know how to be happy in them. He decides that enough is enough and that it's time to teach her a lesson by sexually assaulting her.

1. How much do problems with intimate relationships play a role in your daily life?

0	1	2	3	4	5	6	7	8	9	10
Not at all					Somewhat					A lot

2. How much have problems with intimate relationships played a role in your being able to meet your life goals?

0	1	2	3	4	5	6	7	8	9	10
Not at all					Somewhat					A lot

3. How much have problems with intimate relationships played a role in your non-sexual offending?

0	1	2	3	4	5	6	7	8	9	10
Not at all					Somewhat					A lot

4. How much have problems with intimate relationships played a role in your sexual offending?

0	1	2	3	4	5	6	7	8	9	10
Not at all					Somewhat					A lot

5. Provide below a short description of some of the ways that your problems with intimate relationships play a role in your offending or cause problems meeting your life goals. Please be specific.

____

____

____

____

____

Emotional Connection with Children. Emotional connection is when one person feels in tune and aligned with another person. Some sexual offenders feel closer to children than to other adults—something that is called emotional connection (or congruence) with children. This feeling can lead people to view children as being more psychologically mature than they actually are (and therefore as acceptable sexual partners). This comfort with children also happens when adults themselves feel child-like and are, as a result, more comfortable with children than they are with adults. Sometimes people who are emotionally connected to children view themselves as unusual, isolated, or even inadequate. Often, they feel that children understand them better than adults do. For example, imagine a person who feels that other adults can't understand him as well as children do. He feels lonely in the adult world, and may want to surround himself with children or engage in child-type activities in order to not be lonely. When he is with children, he also develops sexual urges and the desire to be intimate with the children, which leads to sexual abuse.

1. How much does emotional connection with children play a role in your daily life?

0	1	2	3	4	5	6	7	8	9	10
Not at all					Somewhat					A lot

2. How much has emotional connection with children played a role in your non-sexual offending?

0	1	2	3	4	5	6	7	8	9	10
Not at all					Somewhat					A lot

3. How much has emotional connection with children played a role in your sexual offending?

0	1	2	3	4	5	6	7	8	9	10
Not at all					Somewhat					A lot

4. Provide below a short description of some of the ways emotional connection with children plays a role in your offending or creates problems meeting your goals. Please be specific.

____

____

____

____

____

Other Risk Factors

Before moving into the next section of this part of the workbook, it is important to mention some other factors that you may work on in treatment. One is empathy for the victims of your offense(s), which is being able to put yourself into the shoes of people you've hurt or are considering hurting. Many people believe if a person can't imagine the harm his sexual crimes can cause or has already caused his victims, he is more likely to do it again. Another factor is denial of having committed a sexual offense. Many people believe if a person says he didn't commit his crimes, he is at higher risk to do it again. Other people put less importance on this. Certainly, telling the truth about your actions can be a critical part of taking responsibility and making the changes that can then help you to build a better life. Likewise, it may be that not being empathic toward others is already a part of some of the risk factors mentioned above (such as a lack of emotionally intimate relationships). We leave it to you and your therapist to consider where and how these factors fit into your life, your offending, and your planning for the future.

Exercise 4.1: My Risk Factors

Now that you have reviewed all of the risk factors, answer the questions below.

1. Which of the factors have generally been present in your daily life?

____

____

____

____

____

____

Continued on next page

2. Which risk factors have had the biggest influence on your offending, overall?

3. Which risk factors have played a role in your sexual offending?

4. Which risk factors have played a role in your non-sexual offending?

5. What are some other risk factors that you have learned about that were not included in this part of the workbook?

6. What have others identified as the major risk factors that have been present in your daily life?

7. What have others identified as the major risk factors that have contributed to your offending, overall?

8. What have others identified as the major risk factors that have contributed to your sexual offending?

9. What have others identified as the major risk factors that have contributed to your non-sexual offending?

10. How have these risk factors interfered with the common life goals you have tried to achieve?

____

____

____

____

____

____

____

____

____

____

Putting the Pieces Together: Risk Factors and Common Life Goals

How are risk factors and common life goals connected? As you learned earlier, according to the good lives model, the pursuit of goals is an activity all humans share. Risk factors come from those patterns in your life that occur when your efforts to meet goals don't work out or when your attempts make it likely you will offend. This section explores some possibilities for how risk factors are connected with common life goals.

Because it would be impossible to link all possible risk factors to all of the common life goals, below are some examples to show how goals and risk factors can be connected. Your own risk factors are connected to common life goals in unique ways, which you will explore in the next exercise and with your therapist. Here are some examples:

Life: Living and Surviving. In order to support themselves financially, some people commit crimes. Over time, committing crimes can become a pattern for them as well as the means to meet their goals of living and surviving. Risk factors related to this goal might include crime-related schemas or antisocial peers or associates. Examples of crime-related schemas can include the belief that stealing is an acceptable way to meet the goal of life.

Knowledge: Learning and Knowing. Some people commit crimes because they don't have the knowledge about other ways to live. The goal of knowledge or a lack of knowledge may be linked to risk factors such as a lack of self-regulation. When a person has little knowledge of how to manage his emotional states, that lack of knowledge can lead directly to offending. Another knowledge-deficit behavior is when someone uses sex as a coping strategy because he has little knowledge of other ways to cope with stress or emotions. Using sex as a coping tool could also be linked to a lack of emotionally intimate relationships, for example, when someone simply does not know how to form relationships.

Being Good at Work and Play. Some people have few opportunities to feel good about themselves outside of pursuing harmful sexual behavior. Their attempts to be good at work or play come into conflict with other goals that they have in life. Risk factors that can be linked to the goal of being good at work and play include attitudes or schemas that are supportive of committing crimes such as stealing. Similarly, coercive sexual behavior might be one of the few things that a person feels he is good at if he is not satisfied in his job or does not feel he is good at other things.

Personal Choice and Independence. Some people may commit crimes because they feel they have little choice. They may lack the capacity to live differently. Risk factors linked to this goal may include sexual interest in coercion or rape. For example, the person may believe the only way to have a sense of personal control is through abuse. Other risk factors can include resistance to rules and supervision, for example, when a person decides that no one can tell him what to do and as a result, he then commits a crime; or crime-related schemas such as sexual entitlement, for example, "I will decide for myself when to have sex."

Peace of Mind. Some people may engage in crime in the hope it will bring them peace of mind. These people may have no other means for being free of emotional turmoil. Risk factors linked to this life goal can include using sex to cope with stress in order to get peace of mind or to deal with emotions. It also can include emotional connection to children or sexual interest in children—for example, when the person feels more at peace with children than adults and gets peace of mind through having sex with them.

Relationships and Friendships. The pursuit of friendships and relationships can sometimes lead to committing crimes. This goal can come into conflict with the pursuit of other goals, or the person can lack the means for obtaining this goal outside of criminal behavior. Risk factors that may be linked to this goal include *sexual preoccupation* (pursuing sexual relationships at all costs) and *sexual interest* in children, for example, viewing children as ideal sexual partners. Other risk factors can include a lack of emotionally intimate relationships (and the use of offending as a way to obtain those relationships), emotional connection with children, or being a member of a gang in order to have close relationships.

Community: Being Part of a Group. Some people maintain friendships with other people who are sex offenders. These people believe they are among the few people who can understand them. Feeling this way could be a lack of scope in achieving the goal of community, and it also limits these people's community to others who commit sexual crimes. In some cases, people have formed organizations dedicated to having sex with children, and they get a sense of community from this group. Some people belong to gangs in order to feel part of a group. Both of these are the risk factors of *pro-criminal* or *pro-abuse* peers and associates and are also sure to result in *abuse-supportive attitudes and schemas.*

Spirituality: Having Meaning in Life. Some people believe they have no other way to find meaning in life other than through sex or sexual offending. This belief reflects a lack of capacity or means to achieve this goal in other ways. One risk factor linked to this goal might be personality. For example, a person might believe that few things give him a sense of meaning and purpose in life. The only life that a person with this perspective thinks he is good at is one of crime or sexual abuse. The person may even say, "I've tried everything else and been unable to quit. This must just be who I am."

Happiness. Some people are not able to experience happiness other than through activities like crime or sexual abuse. Being unable to experience happiness outside of crime or abuse can reflect problems with capacity, means, or scope. Or, a person could get a sense of pride, satisfaction, or happiness from having gotten away with illegal activity. Some people even feel a sense of accomplishment after committing a sex crime, for example, "She deserved it"; or, "I teach children about the ways of the world by introducing them to sex." Sometimes, people define happiness only as sex or as relationships, which affects their ability to meet this goal in other ways.

Creativity. The goal of creativity can be linked to risk factors such as general self-regulation or sexual preoccupations. Some people who feel a need for new and exciting things in their lives may end up engaging in risky behavior or may become dissatisfied sexually unless the sexual activity feels more and more exciting. This goal may be linked to the risk factors of multiple sexual interests. For example, some people find creativity in unusual sexual behaviors.

To look at an example of the links between common life goals and risk factors, let's return to a case example from chapter 3.

Recall that Chris never had the opportunities that many of his friends had. His father left the family when Chris was still young. After Chris got in trouble a number of times, he attended many different treatment programs. While most other youth his age led happier and more normal lives, Chris had a sexual interest in children. He masturbated a lot before he went to work in the hope that he would become less aroused when he saw children and also so that he could manage his stress levels. Chris also looked at pornography almost every night. This activity didn't help Chris, and, in fact, he found that his urges occurred more and more frequently. Chris told himself, "I've tried everything I can do to not approach those kids. Maybe being attracted to children is simply who I am. Nothing seems to make me less interested in them."

Although this example is short, some risk factors are obvious in Chris's case. He is sexually interested in children, and he is also sexually preoccupied (which is evident in his frequent use of pornography and his high levels of masturbation). He uses sex as a strategy to cope with his stress and emotions, and he has trouble having emotionally intimate relationships with adults. Using sex as a coping strategy and having trouble with intimate relationships can also lead to problems trying to get peace of mind. He also has a schema that it is okay to have sex with children, and his belief that he can't stop is a cognitive distortion. Chris's sexual interest in children is related to the common life goals of happiness, pleasure, and relatedness. That is, he tries to get happiness, pleasure, and relationships with children, and not having intimate relationships with adults also gets in the way of his goals of happiness, pleasure, and relationships. His risk factors may be related to the goal of knowledge because he seems to have little knowledge about how to have relationships with adults.

Next, let's consider the case of the case of Tyler, who sexually assaulted a woman while driving her home from a date. Prior to this offense, Tyler had not been involved in many relationships with women. He blamed his offense on his belief that women are deceitful and difficult to know in any real way. He knew that the woman he asked out had been sexually involved with other men, and so he felt she would be willing to have sex with him, as well. He believed that he was a "very sexual person" with more sexual needs and desires than the average man. When the woman said that she liked him but did not want to spend the night with him, he became intensely angry. Without giving it much thought, he cursed her out and forced her to have sex with him even though she was crying as it happened.

Tyler's risk factors include his abuse-related schemas of sexual entitlement, his belief that women are deceitful, and his belief that he is a "very sexual person" (represented by his sexual preoccupation and his uncontrollable sexual urges). He also has the cognitive distortion that because the woman had been involved with other men sexually, she would want to have sex with Tyler as well. When he doesn't get what he wants, in this or in other situations, Tyler's behavior can be quite impulsive. Tyler also has a lack of emotionally intimate relationships with adults, even though he would like to be more competent in his relationships with them. Because of these risk factors, Tyler tried to meet his life goals of relationships and happiness through forced sex.

In the next exercise, you will look at the link between your risk factors and your common life goals.

Exercise 4.2: My Goals and Risk Factors

In the table that follows, you will find each of the 10 common life goals listed. If you need a reminder of these goals, go back to the Common Life Goals chart on pages 22–25. Next, review all of the risk factors described above and think about which risk factors were related to your offending in meeting each of those life goals. In the second column, write your own risk factors that are related to that life goal. For example, if you get depressed when you are not able to get a job, you would write "depression" as your risk factor for the goal of being good at play and work. Or, if you use alcohol or drugs to cope with stress and that is a risk factor to offend, you would write "substance use" next to the life goal of peace of mind. Lastly, in the third column, write a short description of the link between the risk factor and the life goal. For example, "Because I believed I could have sex whenever I wanted it, I ignored my victim when he/she said 'no' and assaulted her."

Try to fill in risk factors for every life goal. You have no limit on the number of risk factors for each common life goal; the number of risk factors will be unique to you. Some of your life goals may not be linked to risk factors, and some risk factors may be linked to more than one life goal. This is a hard exercise, so be sure to work closely with your therapist because it is an important exercise.

COMMON LIFE GOAL	Life: Living and Surviving (Being healthy and meeting basic needs)
RISK FACTORS	LINKS BETWEEN GOAL AND RISK FACTORS

COMMON LIFE GOAL	Knowledge: Learning and Knowing (Seeking knowledge or information, wanting to learn new things)
RISK FACTORS	LINKS BETWEEN GOAL AND RISK FACTORS

Continued on next page

COMMON LIFE GOAL Being Good at Work and Play (Being good at work or leisure activities)	
RISK FACTORS	LINKS BETWEEN GOAL AND RISK FACTORS

COMMON LIFE GOAL Personal Choice and Independence (Being independent and making one's own way in life)	
RISK FACTORS	LINKS BETWEEN GOAL AND RISK FACTORS

COMMON LIFE GOAL Peace of Mind (Emotional balance, staying calm and relaxed, reducing stress)	
RISK FACTORS	LINKS BETWEEN GOAL AND RISK FACTORS

COMMON LIFE GOAL Relationships and Friendships (Time with family, friends, intimate partners)	
RISK FACTORS	LINKS BETWEEN GOAL AND RISK FACTORS

Continued on next page

COMMON LIFE GOAL Community: Being Part of a Group (Being part of a specific group, belonging to a group, feeling a sense of belonging)	
RISK FACTORS	LINKS BETWEEN GOAL AND RISK FACTORS

COMMON LIFE GOAL Spirituality: Having Meaning in Life (Having purpose and meaning in life)	
RISK FACTORS	LINKS BETWEEN GOAL AND RISK FACTORS

COMMON LIFE GOAL	Happiness (Being content and happy in life, having satisfaction, pleasure, sexual pleasure)
RISK FACTORS	LINKS BETWEEN GOAL AND RISK FACTORS

COMMON LIFE GOAL	Creativity (Trying new things, looking for excitement)
RISK FACTORS	LINKS BETWEEN GOAL AND RISK FACTORS

Continued on next page

Looking back at your answers from the chart, what patterns do you see in the links between your life goals and your own risk factors?

____

____

____

____

____

____

____

____

____

____

Summary

In this part of the workbook, you have learned about risk factors that research shows are related to sexual offending and about how these specific factors apply to you. You have also learned how the factors are connected to common life goals, and what your links are between them. In the next part of the workbook, you will explore your life and learn more about how you have tried to meet your life goals.

CHAPTER 5

My Personal History

Part of treatment usually involves talking about your personal history and doing an "autobiography." The purpose is not to tell your entire life story, but to look at specific events that have happened in your life and to understand how those events have led you to be the person you are today. This process includes looking at both positive and problematic aspects of who you are. For example, some life events strengthen people, making them strong or resilient so they are better able to cope with life's problems and better able to make their way in the world. Other life events can cause problems later in life and can result in a person not being able to meet his goals or to problematic behavior and offending. In short, the life you have lived shapes who you are.

This part of the workbook is designed to help you discover and understand the life events that have made you who you are today, including what you do, how you think, how you react to life situations, how you respond emotionally, and what your attitudes and beliefs are. In this part of the workbook, you will be doing a series of exercises to look at and learn about those factors. In addition, your therapist may ask you to present your autobiography to him or her or to your treatment group. The purpose of sharing your story is to allow you to get feedback from others, and to help you to understand patterns and see where you might need to change parts of your life, your thinking, and your behavior.

You may have participated in treatment before, and you may have been asked to do an autobiography exercise. In this workbook, however, doing your personal history will be different from what you might have done before in a number of ways. First, this exercise will be more focused. You will not be asked to write your life story from beginning to end. Instead, your assignments will be very specific and look at key events in your life. Second, you will be looking not only at events in your life that led you to offend, but also at events that have shaped your good life plan and your self-regulation. You will also look at your risk factors and your strengths.

When people think about change, they often examine their lives and their experiences and discover that events that happened to them in the past still are influencing how they behave and feel today. For example, people who have been abused or neglected as children may end up having problems forming healthy attachments and relationships in their adult life. They may be fearful or suspicious of others' motives or worried that others will hurt them. Sometimes, they come to believe that abuse and neglect are "normal" ways of treating people. Because some people believe that their own abuse "wasn't so bad," they end up harming others because of this belief or attitude and because of not recognizing the impact of abusive behavior.

People can also believe that they are destined by their pasts to have ongoing problems as adults. But, with treatment, this does not have to be true. It is important to point out that not everyone who goes through similar experiences will have the exact same response to those experiences. For example, many people who grow up in homes where there was substance abuse do not go on to abuse drugs and alcohol. Likewise, just because certain experiences made offending more likely in the past, it does not necessarily mean that they will continue to influence people for the rest of their lives.

How Life Events Influence People in the Present

Life events from the past and their influence on people in the present can result in specific problems.

Past events may have the effect of *predisposing* a person to specific life problems. This predisposition means that the person may be more likely than other people to have certain problems in his life. For example: Someone whose parents were alcoholics may be more likely to have problems with substance abuse in his life than is a person whose parents did not abuse substances.

A person can develop specific ways of relating to others based on previous life events. For example, someone who saw his father abusing his mother may be more likely to abuse his own partner than will people who did not grow up exposed to such abuse.

Life events can lead to problems with the ways people think and with the attitudes they develop. For example, a person who was abused or bullied as a child may learn to believe that the world is a hostile place and that he has to "get others before they get him." This attitude can lead that person to misinterpret other people's motives and even to be aggressive toward others.

Life events can contribute to the belief that sexual aggression is okay. For example, a person who was sexually abused himself can reach the conclusion that sexual abuse is a "normal," common, and acceptable way to get sexual pleasure or personal power. He can continue to hold this belief even when he knows it is against the law and even when he is told that it is harmful.

Life events as well as people's physical make-up can lead to problems with self-regulation and with managing emotions, thinking, and behavior. For example, some types of brain injuries can cause a person to become impulsive and unable to control anger and aggression. As another example, when a person does not learn early in life to control his desires and urges, this lack of control can result in the person being impulsive or having trouble planning ahead.

Life events shape people's good life plans and the goals they have in life. For example, a person who grew up in a home where people strongly valued family relationships may form the goal of becoming a good husband and father. A person who grew up in a family with a strong work ethic may highly value knowledge and being good at work.

Life events can also contribute to the problems people have implementing their good life plans (i.e., the flaws of ways to meet goals (means), narrow scope of good life plan, conflict between goals, lack of skills, and lack of opportunities described in chapter 2). Sometimes, earlier in life, people have good life plans, but over time they give up on their plans because those plans didn't work out. These people end up not having a good life, or they change their good life plans many times because they are searching for what they want to get out of life, but they aren't getting what they want or need. For example, a person who grows up disadvantaged and who does not have many opportunities in life may not have many goals in life (which can lead to a very narrow good life plan) because he believes he will not be able to meet his important goals.

Life events can lead to the development of risk factors for sexual offending, described in chapter 4, and to sexual aggression. For example, a person who grows up seeing a lot of sex or sexual abuse can come to put too much importance on sexual pleasure, resulting in a problematic life goal as well as in sexually compulsive behavior.

Life events can lead to risk factors being part of people's good life plan. For example. Most people want to be connected to others and to feel pleasure. A person who has grown up isolated and rejected by others may try to cope with the stresses of daily life by masturbating. Over time, this activity may become his only means of feeling pleasure or relieving stress. This activity can become a more serious risk factor when the person becomes increasingly stressed or when this is the main or only way they feel pleasure or cope with stress or emotions. Here is an example:

> *Michael grew up in a home in which his father sexually abused his sisters in front of his mother and him. His father even made him have sex with his youngest sister. In those days, Michael did not fully understand how these incidents were abusive, and he grew up a scared and lonely young man. He now remembers the time in his life when he realized that other families weren't like his, and didn't have sex with each other. This realization made him even lonelier and angrier. Although Michael never*

enjoyed the incidents of sexual abuse he encountered as a child, he remembered them as being among the few times he ever felt close to anybody.

Unfortunately, Michael continued his abuse of his sister. As a teenager, his past abuse was a predisposing factor toward further sexual aggression. For much of his early teen years, he believed that it was okay to abuse. He held this belief even though he knew the activity was uncommon (other young men he knew didn't have sex with their sisters), but he thought it was acceptable to continue. His past abuse and his isolated upbringing also led to Michael's having few other ways of relating to people. When Michael was trying to achieve the common life goals of pleasure and connection to others, he thought that forcing his sister to have sex with him seemed like the only way possible.

By the time he was in his mid-teens, it became clear to Michael that his behavior was unacceptable and wrong. For the next several years, he worked to have appropriate relationships with others, but he continued to try to force other people to have sex with him even when he knew they didn't want to. Just as his father viewed himself as being entitled to have sex whenever he wanted it, so did Michael. An important part of Michael's good life plan, now that he is in treatment, is to develop new ways to work toward the goals of pleasure and relatedness without causing harm to others.

This example shows how life circumstances can contribute to a pattern of sexual aggression. In this instance, Michael grew up in an abusive home. He regularly saw abuse occur, and so he grew up thinking that relationships between people, especially sexual ones, were abusive and okay. He had also developed other unhealthy schemas about sexuality and relationships. Over time, he came to understand that this behavior was wrong. He had learned a *sexual entitlement schema* from his father, however, and this schema became a lens through which Michael viewed relationships as well as a pattern in his own sexual relationships. Michael would have preferred to have consenting sex, but this schema, along with a history of seeking relatedness and pleasure through inappropriate means, placed him at risk for continued sexual aggression.

Many different life events shape who people become. Those life events also influence their good life plans and their risk factors. People follow life paths for many different reasons that can eventually lead to not having a good life or to offending. In fact, researchers look at many factors, such as genetics, the brain, problems in childhood, and relationships with others throughout life, which can lead to problematic attitudes, deviant sexual interests, problems with self-regulation, and to offending. The important point to remember is that, through change and treatment and support from others, all of these factors can be managed, and you can have a good life and manage your risk in the future. The exercises in this part of the workbook will help you explore the factors that have contributed to your behavior so you can develop a good life plan and a risk management plan. Please keep in mind that because this exercise is just a starting point, your therapist may ask you to do the exercise more than once, in order to help you have a more complete understanding of who you are and how you became the person you are.

Exercise 5.1: My Life in Brief

This first exercise you will do is a general exploration of your life. The purpose is to describe your development until you get to who you are today. The exercise should be relatively short, but it should cover what is important in your background. When working on this exercise, think about the points described above—what shaped your good life plan, your self-regulation, and your risk factors. Use extra paper if you need to. Remember, this exercise should be short but thorough. Think about your answers as if you were talking to a new friend or doing a first background interview with a therapist or probation officer who wants to know who you are and where you came from. Below you will find an example that should help you see the direction you need to go as you work on this exercise:

> *My name is Javier. I was adopted from South America when I was about one year old. I was told that the police had to come and take my sister and me away from my biological mother, because she was some kind of criminal and had a drug problem. I've never known for sure, though. I mention all this because we were adopted by our parents, and we lived in a really nice neighborhood. There's really no reason I should have gotten into all the trouble I did when I was a kid. My sister never did. She graduated from college and is married and has a really good job.*
>
> *The thing about the neighborhood I grew up in is that it was really quiet. My mom and dad worked all the time. He ran a business, and she was a social worker. The earliest memory I have is of all the machinery at my dad's business. He was always talking to customers when I wanted to talk to him. My mom always seemed really strict with the rules. I think that's because she had a lot to do. It always seemed like the times I loved her the most were the times she didn't notice me. She was always getting angry at me and yelling at me. She would send me to my room, and all that. I also got sick a lot when I was a little kid, and she would be mad, because she had to stay home from work to take care of me.*
>
> *Because of my name and my background, I didn't fit in well at my school. Other kids picked on me, and I couldn't handle it. It was just kid stuff, but I couldn't handle it. It hurt. I used to spend a lot of time alone or with my sister. We were really close in those days. We used to play house, and when we were young we used to play like we were having sex sometimes. I started pushing her hard to have sex when I was 11*

years old. The short version is that I couldn't get along with the other kids, but I really wanted to find out what sex was like. The first time I finally got my sister to agree, it felt really great. Afterward, I couldn't believe I'd done that, and I knew it was wrong. I mean, this was my sister! But that feeling of finally getting my way for once was like a drug, and I just wanted to keep going.

When I was 12, I decided I'd had enough of being picked on at school. One day during recess when a whole bunch of guys were around, a kid from a grade below me got in my face. I wasn't going to stand for that, so I punched him really hard. He got a bloody nose and his glasses went flying. I got suspended for a week. My parents got really angry with me, and that's when my sister told that I'd been abusing her, as well.

I went to a foster home, and that's the last I remember of anything going right in my life. I didn't do well there, I missed my family, and I did terribly in the school. In that new school, I got picked on even more than before. The school always had someone supervising me, and that made a bad situation worse.

I went back to live with my family when I was 15. I went back to the same school and by then I had gotten to know some guys who were always getting high. They were good guys, but they sure did get high a lot. It didn't take me too long to get arrested while I was out partying with them. It never seemed fair that I was always getting into trouble when everyone seemed to be doing the same stuff and getting away with it.

Looking back, I abandoned a lot of good life goals. I could have been creative about meeting girls. I could have sought more knowledge. These things would have also helped me figure out the best way to establish relationships. I'm actually a good-looking Latino guy, but I told myself, "I'm no good" and also said, "Why bother trying? I'm never going to get what I want." I had a belief that I was entitled to get what I wanted even if I didn't work for it. A really important goal of mine was happiness and pleasure. I always used to think that sex was the only way to feel good. Since then, I've learned that I can accomplish a lot just by keeping in shape. Nowadays, I want to use my time in treatment to get better at pursuing creativity and knowledge so that I don't have to be so hard on myself and others ever again. I don't ever want to hurt anyone again.

As this example shows, Javier never developed the skills to form healthy relationships when he was younger. As he matured and naturally became more interested in sex, his good life plan of happiness and pleasure came into conflict with many of his other goals, such as relationships and personal choice. He also sought happiness mostly through sex (which represented a problem with *means*), even though he knew this approach was wrong. He tried to get peace of mind through drugs and sex. His schemas supported this choice and also caused him to give up on other life goals, such as knowledge and creativity. His drive toward happiness and pleasure had always been very strong, but it led to a risk factor of sexual entitlement.

Summary of My Life

For this first exercise, write about your development up until you get to who you are today. What you write should be relatively short, but it should cover what is important in your background—what shaped your good life plan, your self-regulation, and your risk factors. Use extra paper if you need to. Remember, this exercise is only an overview. But, it is important to focus on the specific, important areas of your life that have led to offending, risk, and problems with your good life plan.

Continued on next page

Exercise 5.2: My Early Good Life Plans

In chapter 2, you looked at your good life plan and your life goals right now that make up that plan. You also learned that people's good life plans change over time. This next exercise is about understanding what your good life plan was at various stages when you were younger—when you were a child, a teenager, and a young adult. You can also add any other timeframe for your life that has been important in the formation of your good life plans. The purpose here is to understand what your good life plan was at each of these times, to look at the goals you had then that have lasted until the present time, and to remember any goals you might have given up on because you felt you wouldn't or couldn't attain them.

For your review, here are the 10 common life goals that make up a balanced good life plan:

- *Life: Living and Surviving.* This goal is important to people who think about or spend time being healthy or making sure they are able to meet their basic needs.
- *Knowledge: Learning and Knowing.* This goal is important to people who think about or spend time seeking knowledge or information.
- *Being Good at Work and Play.* This goal is important to people who think about or spend time trying to be good at work or leisure activities.
- *Personal Choice and Independence.* This goal is important to people who think about or spend time being independent and making their own way in life.
- *Peace of Mind.* This goal is important to people who think about or spend time trying to be calm and relaxed, or time trying to reduce stress and its effects in their lives.
- *Relationships and Friendships.* This goal is important to people who think about or spend time with family, friends, or romantic partners.
- *Community: Being Part of a Group.* This goal is important to people who think about or spend time being a part of a specific group of people.
- *Spirituality: Having Meaning in Life.* This goal is important to people who think about or spend time looking for a purpose or meaning in life.
- *Happiness.* This goal is important to people who think about or spend time wanting to be content or happy, or to experience pleasure.
- *Creativity.* This goal is important to people who think about or spend time creating or trying new things or looking for excitement.

First, start with the following questions:

1. When you were younger, what did you long for? What were your hopes and dreams about your life when you were younger?

2. Who or what did you dream of becoming?

3. Who was your hero or your idol when you were young? Did you have more than one hero or idol? Why did that person or those persons stand out to you?

4. What was missing from your life when you were a child? When you were a teenager?

5. When times were hard as a child or as a teenager, what did you wish would happen, or what did you want to change?

For this next part, consider the 10 common life goals that make up a good life plan and answer the following questions for all 10 goals separately. When you are finished, you will summarize your three early good life plans—as a child, as a teenager, and as a young adult.

Life: Living and Surviving

1. How important was living and surviving to you as a child? As a teenager? As a young adult? Was it something you really wanted or something you didn't care so much about?
2. How important to making your life good was living and surviving at that time of your life?
3. What did you do that worked to live and to survive?
4. What did you do that did not work so well to live and to survive?
5. How important was living and surviving to the people around you, such as your parents, brothers and sisters, and friends?
6. Did you think you could meet this goal then, or was it something you thought you could never get?
7. Did anyone around you have any of the four problems/flaws to live and survive? Who were they (their relationship to you) and how did they show these problems?
8. How was living and surviving related to any life problems at that time of your life?
9. How was living and surviving related to any of your sexual or other offenses at that time of your life?

Knowledge: Learning and Knowing

1. How important was learning and knowledge to you as a child? As a teenager? As a young adult? Was it something you really wanted or something you didn't care so much about?
2. How important to making your life good was learning and knowledge at that time of your life?
3. What did you do that worked to help you to learn and gain knowledge?
4. What did you do that did not work so well to help you to learn and to gain knowledge?
5. How important was learning and knowledge to the people around you, such as your parents, brothers and sisters, and friends?
6. Did you think you could meet this goal then, or was it something you thought you could never get?
7. Did anyone around you have any of the four problems/flaws related to this goal? Who were they (their relationship to you) and how did they show these problems?
8. How was learning or a lack of knowledge related to any life problems at that time of your life?
9. How was learning or a lack of knowledge related to any of your sexual or other offenses at that time of your life?

Being Good at Work and Play

1. How important was being good at work or at play to you as a child? As a teenager? As a young adult? Was it something you really wanted or something you didn't care so much about?
2. How important to making your life good was being good at work or at play at that time of your life?
3. What did you do that worked to help you to be good at work or at play?
4. What did you do that did not work so well to help you to be good at work or at play?
5. How important was being good at work or at play to the people around you, such as your parents, brothers and sisters, and friends?
6. Did you think you could meet this goal then, or was it something you thought you could never get?
7. Did anyone around you have any of the four problems/flaws related to this goal? Who were they (their relationship to you) and how did they show these problems?
8. How was not being good at work or at play related to any life problems at that time of your life?
9. How was not being good at work or at play related to any of your sexual or other offenses at that time of your life?

Personal Choice and Independence

1. How important was personal choice or being independent to you as a child? As a teenager? As a young adult? Was it something you really wanted or something you didn't care so much about?
2. How important to making your life good was personal choice or being independent at that time of your life?
3. What did you do that worked to help you to have personal choice or to be independent?
4. What did you do that did not work so well to help you to have personal choice or to be independent?
5. How important was personal choice or being independent to the people around you, such as your parents, brothers and sisters, and friends?
6. Did you think you could meet this goal then, or was it something you thought you could never get?
7. Did anyone around you have any of the four problems/flaws related to this goal? Who were they (their relationship to you) and how did they show these problems?
8. How was personal choice or being independent related to any life problems at that time of your life?
9. How was personal choice or being independent related to any of your sexual or other offenses at that time of your life?

Peace of Mind

1. How important was having peace of mind to you as a child? As a teenager? As a young adult? Was it something you really wanted or something you didn't care so much about?
2. How important to making your life good was having peace of mind at that time of your life?
3. What did you do that worked to help you to have peace of mind?
4. What did you do that did not work so well to help you to have peace of mind?
5. How important was having peace of mind to the people around you, such as your parents, brothers and sisters, and friends?
6. Did you think you could meet this goal then, or was it something you thought you could never get?
7. Did anyone around you have any of the four problems/flaws related to this goal? Who were they (their relationship to you) and how did they show these problems?
8. How was trying to have peace of mind related to any life problems at that time of your life?
9. How was trying to have peace of mind related to any of your sexual or other offenses at that time of your life?

Relationships and Friendships

1. How important was having relationships and friendships to you as a child? As a teenager? As a young adult? Was it something you really wanted or something you didn't care so much about?
2. How important to making your life good was having relationships and friendships at that time of your life?
3. What did you do that worked to help you to have relationships and friendships?
4. What did you do that did not work so well to help you to have relationships and friendships?
5. How important was having relationships and friendships to the people around you, such as your parents, brothers and sisters, and friends?
6. Did you think you could meet this goal then, or was it something you thought you could never get?
7. Did anyone around you have any of the four problems/flaws related to this goal? Who were they (their relationship to you) and how did they show these problems?
8. How was trying to have relationships and friendships related to any life problems at that time of your life?
9. How was trying to have relationships and friendships related to any of your sexual or other offenses at that time of your life?

Community: Being Part of a Group

1. How important was being part of a group to you as a child? As a teenager? As a young adult? Was it something you really wanted or something you didn't care so much about?
2. How important to making your life good was being part of a group at that time of your life?
3. What did you do that worked to help you to be part of a group?
4. What did you do that did not work so well to help you to be part of a group?
5. How important was it to be part of a group to the people around you, such as your parents, brothers and sisters, and friends?
6. Did you think you could meet this goal then, or was it something you thought you could never get?
7. Did anyone around you have any of the four problems/flaws related to this goal? Who were they (their relationship to you) and how did they show these problems?
8. How was trying to be part of a group related to any life problems at that time of your life?
9. How was trying to be part of a group related to any of your sexual or other offenses at that time of your life?

Spirituality: Having Meaning in Life

1. How important was having meaning in your life to you as a child? As a teenager? As a young adult? Was it something you really wanted or something you didn't care so much about?
2. How important to making your life good was having meaning in your life at that time of your life?
3. What did you do that worked to help you to have meaning in your life?
4. What did you do that did not work so well to help you to have meaning in your life?
5. How important was having meaning in life to the people around you, such as your parents, brothers and sisters, and friends?
6. Did you think you could meet this goal then, or was it something you thought you could never get?
7. Did anyone around you have any of the four problems/flaws related to this goal? Who were they (their relationship to you) and how did they show these problems?
8. How was trying to have meaning in your life related to any life problems at that time of your life?
9. How was trying to have meaning in your life related to any of your sexual or other offenses at that time of your life?

Happiness

1. How important was having happiness, contentment, and pleasure to you as a child? As a teenager? As a young adult? Was it something you really wanted or something you didn't care so much about?
2. How important to making your life good was having happiness, contentment, and pleasure at that time of your life?
3. What did you do that worked to help you to have happiness, contentment, and pleasure in your life?
4. What did you do that did not work so well to help you to have happiness, contentment, and pleasure in your life?
5. How important was having happiness, contentment, and pleasure in life to the people around you, such as your parents, brothers and sisters, and friends?
6. Did you think you could meet this goal then, or was it something you thought you could never get?
7. Did anyone around you have any of the four problems/flaws related to this goal? Who were they (their relationship to you) and how did they show these problems?
8. How was trying to have happiness, contentment, and pleasure in your life related to any life problems at that time of your life?
9. How was trying to have happiness, contentment, and pleasure in your life related to any of your sexual or other offenses at that time of your life?

Creativity

1. How important was having creativity in your life to you as a child? As a teenager? As a young adult? Was it something you really wanted or something you didn't care so much about?
2. How important to making your life good was having creativity in your life at that time of your life?
3. What did you do that worked to help you to have creativity in your life?
4. What did you do that did not work so well to help you to have creativity in your life?
5. How important was having creativity in life to the people around you, such as your parents, brothers and sisters, and friends?
6. Did you think you could meet this goal then, or was it something you thought you could never get?
7. Did anyone around you have any of the four problems/flaws related to this goal? Who were they (their relationship to you) and how did they show these problems?
8. How was trying to have creativity in your life related to any life problems at that time of your life?
9. How was trying to have creativity in your life related to any of your sexual or other offenses at that time of your life?

My Early Good Life Plan as a Child

Thinking about your answers to all of the questions above, write a brief summary of your early good life plan when you were a child.

My Early Good Life Plan as a Teenager

Thinking about your answers to all of the questions above, write a brief summary of your early good life plan when you were a teenager.

My Early Good Life Plan as a Young Adult

Thinking about your answers to all of the questions above, write a brief summary of your early good life plan when you were a young adult.

Summary of Patterns in My Early Good Life Plans

In looking at the different stages of your life—childhood, adolescence, and young adulthood—what patterns do you see? For example, did your goals stay the same or did they change over time? What flaws did you have in your good life plans that led to life problems and to offending? What risk factors do you see? Did you try the same strategies—the *ways* or *means*—all the time, which then led to problems? How do these patterns affect your behavior now? How are your early good life plans related to your good life plan now as an adult? Use extra paper for this exercise if you need to.

Continued on next page

Exercise 5.3: What Is Shaping My Good Life Plan Today

As described above, part of understanding your personal history is knowing the factors that led to who you are today as well as what has led to your life problems and not meeting your goals. In exercise 5.2, you looked at your good life plans at different time periods of your life and at the patterns across these time periods. This next exercise will help you look at the factors and events in your life that led to the development of your goals, your good life plans, your life problems, your risk factors, and your strengths. The idea is to look back on events in your life—and the patterns across your life—so that you are able to see how you got to where you are today.

1. What factors in your family background or where and how you grew up contributed to your good life plans, to your strengths, and to your problems in life?

2. What factors in your relationships with your family members contributed to your good life plans, to your strengths, and to your problems in life?

3. What factors in school contributed to your good life plans, to your strengths, and to your problems in life?

____

____

____

____

____

____

____

____

4. What factors in your relationships with others contributed to your good life plans, to your strengths, and to your problems in life?

____

____

____

____

____

____

____

____

5. What factors in your work contributed to your good life plans, to your strengths, and to your problems in life?

____

____

____

____

6. What factors in your sexual and intimate experiences and relationships contributed to your good life plans, to your strengths, and to your problems in life?

7. What other factors contributed to your good life plans, to your strengths, and to your problems in life?

Summary of What Shaped My Good Life Plans

In looking at your answers for questions 1–7, what patterns do you see?

Exercise 5.4: What Factors Shaped My Offending?

In chapter 4, you looked at your risk factors for offending. This next exercise is to help you look at the factors or life events that led to your offending. You will be addressing your sexual offending, any other type of offending you've done, and any aggression, whether or not you have been convicted for these behaviors.

1. What factors in your family background or where and how you grew up could have contributed to your sexual offending? To any aggressive behavior on your part? To any other types of offending you might have done?

____

____

____

____

____

____

____

____

2. What factors in your relationships in your family could have contributed to your sexual offending? To any aggressive behavior on your part? To any other types of offenses you might have committed?

____

____

____

____

____

____

____

____

3. What factors in school could have contributed to your sexual offending? To any aggressive behavior on your part? To any other types of offending you might have done?

4. What factors in your relationships with others could have contributed to your sexual offending? To any aggressive behavior on your part? To any other types of offending you might have done?

5. What factors in your work could have contributed to your sexual offending? To any aggressive behavior on your part? To any other types of offending you might have done?

6. What factors in your sexual and intimate experiences and relationships could have contributed to your sexual offending? To any aggressive behavior on your part? To any other types of offending you might have done?

7. What other factors could have contributed to your sexual offending? To any aggressive behavior on your part? To any other types of offending you might have done?

Summary of the Factors That Shaped My Offending

In looking at your answers for questions 1–7, what patterns do you see?

Exercise 5.5: Wrap-Up

Now it's time to put the pieces together. In the pages that follow, you will find a large circle for each of the common life goal that you've learned about in this workbook. Write in the circle the key things you have learned about your life story, your early good life plan, the factors that shaped your good life plan up to the present, the factors that shaped your offending, and the ways you might better achieve your goals in the future. By the time you're done, you will have ten circles filled with a short summary of the good and not-so-good things (in other words, the positive and negative things) about your life as well as a sense of where you can go in the future. You can then put the circles on the wall of your room or group room in order to explore your life at a deeper level, by yourself or with your peers. What will you see when you do that? What will others see?

Life: Living and Surviving

Key things that I've learned about my life story, my early good life plans, the factors that have shaped my good life plan to the present, what factors have shaped my offending, and how I might better achieve this goal in the future.

Knowledge: Learning and Knowing

Key things that I've learned about my life story, my early good life plans, the factors that have shaped my good life plan to the present, what factors have shaped my offending, and how I might better achieve this goal in the future.

Being Good at Work and Play

Key things that I've learned about my life story, my early good life plans, the factors that have shaped my good life plan to the present, what factors have shaped my offending, and how I might better achieve this goal in the future.

Personal Choice and Independence

Key things that I've learned about my life story, my early good life plans, the factors that have shaped my good life plan to the present, what factors have shaped my offending, and how I might better achieve this goal in the future.

Peace of Mind

Key things that I've learned about my life story, my early good life plans, the factors that have shaped my good life plan to the present, what factors have shaped my offending, and how I might better achieve this goal in the future.

Relationships and Friendships

Key things that I've learned about my life story, my early good life plans, the factors that have shaped my good life plan to the present, what factors have shaped my offending, and how I might better achieve this goal in the future.

Community: Being Part of a Group

Key things that I've learned about my life story, my early good life plans, the factors that have shaped my good life plan to the present, what factors have shaped my offending, and how I might better achieve this goal in the future.

Spirituality: Having Meaning in Life

Key things that I've learned about my life story, my early good life plans, the factors that have shaped my good life plan to the present, what factors have shaped my offending, and how I might better achieve this goal in the future.

Happiness

Key things that I've learned about my life story, my early good life plan, the factors that have shaped my good life plan to the present, what factors have shaped my offending, and how I might better achieve this goal in the future.

Creativity

Key things that I've learned about my life story, my early good life plans, the factors that have shaped my good life plan to the present, what factors have shaped my offending, and how I might better achieve this goal in the future.

Summary

In this part of the workbook, you have examined your good life plan at different stages of your life. This examination has included looking at the goals that have been most important to you, learning how you have sought to achieve them, looking at the factors that have shaped your good life plan, and seeing better what factors have shaped your offending. Congratulations! You've done some very important work. In the next part of this workbook you will further explore these concepts and learn about their impact on the progression of your offending.

CHAPTER 6

My Offense Chain

In this section, you will look in detail at what happened when you committed your sex offenses. This process will help you to understand exactly what happened so you can stop it from happening again and so you can have a better future.

If you have been in other treatment programs, you may notice two things that are different about this workbook. First, this book uses the word *chain*, instead of *cycle*. The terms *cycle* or *cycle of abuse* suggest that the same thing happens over and over again. This is sometimes true, but not always. Some people's behavior does not always repeat itself the same way over and over again. Instead, people can easily find themselves caught in several different chains of events that then can result in abusive behavior. Second, this book looks not only at your risk factors, but also at how the 10 common life goals are related to your offending behavior. As described earlier, even though you harmed someone through your abusive behavior, your goals may have been appropriate or acceptable, but the *way* you went about meeting those goals (such as by being abusive) was the problem.

As you know by now, sex offending does not "just happen." It results both from a series of events and from the decisions and choices you make when these events happen. In the last section, you learned about aspects of yourself and of your life that make you more likely than other people to commit sexual abuse. These predisposing factors affect how you see others and the world around you, how you react to situations that happen to you, and what decisions you make in those situations. Sometimes, you are not aware of the decisions you make because you make them automatically. Remember the idea of cognitive schemas from chapter 3? These schemas are sets of beliefs and attitudes that help people to understand and respond to what is going on around them. Because a lot can be happening at once, your reactions sometimes might seem to be impulsive or to happen "without thinking." But a lot of thinking and behavior happens without people always being fully aware of what is happening. In this part of the workbook, you will learn about what happens in such situations and how these situations and your reactions can lead to offending.

The offense chain is shown below. This diagram shows the different steps in the chain. The focus in this offense chain is on sexual offending, but you can apply the information you learn about this chain to other offenses, as well.

THE OFFENSE CHAIN

Steps in the Offense Chain

You can see from the diagram that the offense chain has nine steps. After you read about each step below, write down what was happening during your offending. You will have the opportunity to discuss and expand on this assignment with your therapist. You may need to write your offense chain description more than once, if you have committed more than one offense or if your offenses were different. For example, you might have committed sex offenses against three children and also against an adult woman. These two types of offenses are very different from each other, so you may need to complete an offense chain for the offenses against the children and then complete another for the offense against the woman. Your therapist will help you with this process.

The steps in the offense chain are described below. As you read these steps, think about your offenses and about how each step fits with your offending. Remember to do this process for all of your offenses, whether or not you have been convicted for those offenses.

Step 1: Life Event (Early in the Offense Chain)

The offense chain starts with an event—called a *life event*—that starts the chain in motion. It is a starting point that is farther back in time from your offense. The event can be something really important, like losing your job or your partner ending your relationship. Or the event can be something that is not as big or dramatic, but that seemed important when it happened, such as having an argument with someone. This life event provokes or triggers reactions and behavior that later can result in your committing a sex offense or hurting someone. An example is provided here to illustrate this kind of life event:

> *John, a 45-year-old man, has been convicted for rape on three occasions. He had a strict upbringing by his parents and grew up feeling inadequate and worthless. He felt he could never do anything right. He didn't do well in school, and his father was often very critical of him because of his grades. John would have liked a long-term relationship with a woman, but he has never met someone he would like as a partner. John identified these factors as background factors in his personal history.*
>
> *A few months before his first offense, John made an important mistake at work. His boss was very understanding, but John thought he could have done better. John knew that because his parents had been so critical of him, he had become very critical of himself and his mistakes. Regardless, John always tried to do his best at everything. Before he offended for the first time, he focused on his work and was trying to make up for his mistake. He worked extra hours and did extra work. Because of this, he could not go out with his friends, and he didn't feel better about his work, either.*

Can you identify the life event that started John's offense chain?

If you said the life event was the mistake John made at work, you would be right. This mistake built on his feelings of not being good enough, which had developed when he was younger and was a predisposing factor for offending. After making the mistake, John tried to work extra hard, but he wasn't able to get past the mistake he had made and the feeling that he was not good enough. It was very important to him to be good at work—a life goal he was trying to attain. This event started the offense chain in motion.

Exercise 6.1: My Life Event Early in Time

1. Think back to your most recent sex offense and what started your offense chain in motion. This is the life event that started you thinking something was wrong, or maybe you felt that someone had done something wrong to you. Or, it could be that you were thinking you would lose something in your life. It could also be that you were trying to meet a goal in your good life plan. Remember, this event is something that happened long before you offended; you will work on the things that happened immediately before the offense later. You may not have thought this was important at the time, but looking back now, you know it was important. Write what this initial event was below and then you'll begin to see how it started your offense chain.

Life Event That Started the Chain for My Most Recent Offense:

____

____

____

____

2. Now think about your past sex offenses, whether or not you were ever convicted for those offenses. What life events led to those offenses? Those life events may be the same or different from the ones you experienced at the time of your most recent offense. Write below what these early events were. If you have a lot of offenses, write them down on a separate piece of paper. Look for patterns across your offenses; look for offense chains that started with the same type of events. You don't need to write down every life event for every offense you have committed when the offenses are very similar.

Life Event for Past Offense 1:

Life Event for Past Offense 2:

Life Event for Past Offense 3:

Life Event for Past Offense 4:

3. In looking back at your recent and past sex offenses, what life events do you see that are the same? What life events are different?

____

____

____

____

4. Are the life events that started your offense chain different enough that you need to complete more than one offense chain?

   ❐ Yes

   ❐ No

Step 2: Reaction to Life Event

Every time something happens to a person, he reacts or responds to the event in some way. These reactions are why a person's life event can provoke or start an offense chain in motion. Reacting involves what you think, how you feel, and what you do in response. Remember from your work on schemas that the situation is filtered through mental shortcuts. People typically react in ways that are consistent or in line with what they believe about themselves, others, and the world in general. People react to what they think or how they feel about a situation instead of to what actually happens. It is people's *perceptions* and *interpretations* that lead to their reactions, not the situation or the life event itself.

Let's go back to the example of John, described above. Think about the example of John and the life event that started his offense chain. What might John have been saying to himself at the time he made the mistake at work? What were his cognitive schemas, based on his thoughts about what he should do? If you think about it, everyone makes mistakes. The problem was not that John made a mistake, but that he thought about that mistake through the filter of his father's expectations when he was younger. His father's expectations have been accepted by John to use for himself as an adult. So, the problem wasn't making a mistake. It was what John told himself—how he interpreted the event—that created the problem. By having such high expectations for himself, John was very likely to feel bad whenever he made mistakes. So he would focus both on the mistake and on making himself feel better about the mistake. Also, making a mistake had a very big influence on John because, in his good life plan, it was very important to him to be good at work. So, making mistakes signaled to him that he might not meet his life goal and, therefore, the mistake threatened his good life plan.

Exercise 6.2: My Reactions to Life Events

For each of the life events you wrote down in the last exercise, now write down what you were thinking, what you were feeling, and what you did at the time of those events. It is important to really think about how you reacted to the events. It will be helpful if you remember that thoughts, feelings, and behavior sometimes seem to happen automatically.

First, write down the life event or events that started your offense chain in motion, from exercise 6.1. You might have remembered only one event, but you might have recognized more than one, such as when a number of things happen at once. Different life events can trigger different types of offenses. For each life event, write down how you felt about that event. Your feelings could be positive or negative or a combination of both. Next, write what you were thinking when this life event happened, then write what you did when the event happened or immediately after it happened. Do this for all of the different offenses and life events you looked at in exercise 6.1.

LIFE EVENT #1	______________________ ______________________ ______________________
HOW I FELT ABOUT IT	______________________ ______________________ ______________________
WHAT I WAS THINKING DURING OR RIGHT AFTER IT HAPPENED	______________________ ______________________ ______________________
WHAT I DID DURING OR RIGHT AFTER IT HAPPENED	______________________ ______________________ ______________________

Continued on next page

LIFE EVENT #2	
HOW I FELT ABOUT IT	
WHAT I WAS THINKING DURING OR RIGHT AFTER IT HAPPENED	
WHAT I DID DURING OR RIGHT AFTER IT HAPPENED	

LIFE EVENT #3	
HOW I FELT ABOUT IT	

WHAT I WAS THINKING DURING OR RIGHT AFTER IT HAPPENED	
WHAT I DID DURING OR RIGHT AFTER IT HAPPENED	

LIFE EVENT #4	
HOW I FELT ABOUT IT	
WHAT I WAS THINKING DURING OR RIGHT AFTER IT HAPPENED	
WHAT I DID DURING OR RIGHT AFTER IT HAPPENED	

Continued on next page

LIFE EVENT #5	
HOW I FELT ABOUT IT	
WHAT I WAS THINKING DURING OR RIGHT AFTER IT HAPPENED	
WHAT I DID DURING OR RIGHT AFTER IT HAPPENED	

1. In looking back at your recent and past sex offenses and the triggering life events, what reactions to those events are the same and what reactions are different?

2. Are your reactions to the life events that started your offense chain different enough that you need to complete more than one offense chain?

   ❒ Yes
   ❒ No

Step 3: Goals

When something happens and you react to this life event, you make a decision about the goals you want to achieve in the situation. Just like your reactions, the choice of these goals can seem to happen automatically. But actual thought goes into the choices you make. That thinking is often based on your previous experiences, behavior, and schemas. Use this step in this excercise to understand specifically to what you wanted to get out of the situation that was caused by the life event. You might have wanted to achieve a good life goal or an offense goal, or both. Because this kind of goal can lead to offending, it is referred to as an *offense-related goal,* even if it is one of the common life goals.

Let's look again at John's situation from earlier. John's background made him more likely than other people to commit a sex offense. When he made a mistake at work (the life event that started the offense chain), his reaction was to feel bad and to try to feel better. What he usually did when he needed to feel better was to masturbate or to have sex. So, in this situation, John had a few goals: First, he wanted to make up for his mistake so that he could meet his life goal of being good at work. Second, he wanted to feel better and to increase his peace of mind. Third, he wanted to make himself feel better through having sex. So, John had two good life plan goals (work and feeling better), and one goal that was a risk factor related to offending—feeling better by using sex.

Step 4: Strategies to Meet Goals

When you develop goals, the next step is to decide what you need to do to reach the goals. The steps you take toward meeting goals are called *strategies.* Sometimes, these strategies help you to meet your goals, but sometimes they don't work out and you don't meet your goals. Sometimes, you meet some goals but not others, so maybe you are partly successful. Also, sometimes your strategies are *active* and sometimes they are *passive.* When your strategies are *active*, you plan your behavior so you can meet your goals. For example, if one of your goals was to have a relationship with your partner again, your plan and the strategy you use might be to try to talk to him or her in order to re-establish your relationship. Talking to try to work things out is an active strategy. When your strategies are *passive*, you don't plan your behavior as much, or you try to ignore what is happening. For example, you might have become sexually aroused in a situation, but you knew that the arousal was not something you should act on. So you tried to ignore the arousal until it went away. In that instance, you are not really doing anything about the situation. This type of response is known as a *passive strategy*. Or maybe you just acted impulsively, without thinking. This response is also a passive strategy.

Remember John's goals were to make up for his mistake at work, to feel better, and to use sex to feel better. John had two strategies: he worked extra hard in order to make up for his mistake. This was an active strategy. However, he also hoped that he would feel better by doing more work. Relying on hope was a passive strategy that did not work to make him feel better. Third, he ended up going out with a woman, and the situation got out of control, which resulted in John committing rape. John determined he needed the sex to feel better about himself. It did work a bit initially. He felt more relaxed after the sex, but the effects didn't last very long. Seeking out sex and having it end up in a rape was an active strategy because John committed this act with the intention to try to make himself feel better.

In the next exercise, you will write the goals you had and the strategies you used to meet your goals in your offense chain. Even if you weren't aware of the strategies at the time, write them down now so you have the opportunity to think about them. When you are thinking about your strategies, try to think about what types they were—active or passive or both. What is most important in this assignment is to understand *all* of your goals and *all* of your strategies, even if your strategy was to do nothing or even if it didn't work out or made things worse. Your therapist will help you decide if your strategies were active or passive.

Exercise 6.3: My Goals and Strategies

In the chart that follows write down your life events again, and then write down your goals in each situation. Next, write what you did to try to meet your goals (your strategies), and write if these strategies were passive or active.

LIFE EVENT #1	
MY GOAL IN THE SITUATION	

MY STRATEGIES TO MEET MY GOALS	PASSIVE OR ACTIVE

LIFE EVENT #2	
MY GOAL IN THE SITUATION	

MY STRATEGIES TO MEET MY GOALS	PASSIVE OR ACTIVE

Continued on next page

LIFE EVENT #3	
MY GOAL IN THE SITUATION	

MY STRATEGIES TO MEET MY GOALS	PASSIVE OR ACTIVE

LIFE EVENT #4	
MY GOAL IN THE SITUATION	

MY STRATEGIES TO MEET MY GOALS	PASSIVE OR ACTIVE

LIFE EVENT #5	____________________ ____________________ ____________________
MY GOAL IN THE SITUATION	____________________ ____________________ ____________________

MY STRATEGIES TO MEET MY GOALS	PASSIVE OR ACTIVE
____________________	__________
____________________	__________
____________________	__________

1. In looking back at your recent and past sex offenses, which goals and strategies are the same, and which ones are different?

____

____

____

____

____

____

____

2. Are your goals and strategies different enough that you need to complete more than one offense chain?

   ❒ Yes

   ❒ No

Step 5: Situation Right Before Offending

Because of the reactions, goals, and strategies people have and how they decide to act, they will find themselves in situations where they can meet some of their goals. Sometimes, a person finds himself in a *high-risk situation* for offending—a situation where he can meet his goals, but that situation involves high risk for possibly hurting someone or committing an offense. Remember from Step 1, an early event happened that set your offense chain in motion. In Step 5, you are closer to offending—you have already reacted to the life event and you have decided on your goals and strategies. Step 5 is about the situation in which you were closer to offending, so it actually is another event, one that happens later in the offense chain. You may or may not have been thinking about offending, but it was close to happening at that point.

In the example earlier, John ended up committing rape because he wanted to feel better. So, sex was his strategy for feeling better. Here's what happened next:

> *John went to his brother Paul's house and they started drinking, something that also made John feel a bit better, at least at the time. Paul had to go out so at one point, though, so John was left alone with Maria, Paul's girlfriend. To John, she seemed fun and open, so he "came on" to her. She said, "No," and John got angry. All he could think about was feeling better. John tried to talk Maria into having sex, but she kept refusing. John was focused on only his own goals in the situation—having sex and feeling better—so he raped her.*

In this example, what is John's situation before he offended?

John's situation was the following: He was alone with a woman, was coming on to her, and was focusing on his need to feel better. If you were able to view John's situation this way, you identified John's Step 5 event or his high-risk situation. Drinking was also a risk for John in this situation, as well as maybe a sense of entitlement to have sex.

Step 6: Behavior Right Before Offending

The next step for you to think about is what you did in the situation you were in, right before you offended. Remember that by this point, you were in a situation that led to offending, even if you had tried to stop yourself earlier in the chain.

This step also includes what you were thinking and how you were feeling as well as what you did. You may have been thinking everything was okay in the situation—for example, you may have thought you were having consensual sex. Or, you may have been using *cognitive distortions* before you offended. Remember, people use cognitive distortions to give themselves permission to offend, or to justify, or to rationalize what they are about to do. Cognitive distortions help you to convince yourself that it is okay to do what you are going to do, even if it leads to offending. As you know, cognitive distortions are based on your core beliefs and schemas, which you also learned about earlier.

In terms of how you were feeling, you may have been happy, angry, looking forward to offending, or something else. You may not have been feeling empathy for the victim of your offense or thinking about his or her feelings. The important thing about emotions is that people can have many different feelings at the same time. So, when you write about what you were feeling during your offending, write *all* of your emotions, whether they were positive or negative or both.

Exercise 6.4: The Situation and My Behavior Before Offending

Describe the situation right before you offended in the chart below (Step 5 in the offense chain). Write down what you did in the situation, what you were thinking, and how you were feeling (Step 6). If you have committed different types of offenses, write down the different situations and your behavior, thoughts, and feelings for each type of offense.

SITUATION BEFORE OFFENSE #1	______ ______ ______
WHAT I WAS THINKING	______ ______ ______
HOW I WAS FEELING	______ ______ ______
WHAT I DID	______ ______ ______

Continued on next page

SITUATION BEFORE OFFENSE #2	
WHAT I WAS THINKING	
HOW I WAS FEELING	
WHAT I DID	

SITUATION BEFORE OFFENSE #3	
WHAT I WAS THINKING	

HOW I WAS FEELING	
WHAT I DID	

SITUATION BEFORE OFFENSE #4	
WHAT I WAS THINKING	
HOW I WAS FEELING	
WHAT I DID	

Continued on next page

SITUATION BEFORE OFFENSE #5	______ ______ ______
WHAT I WAS THINKING	______ ______ ______
HOW I WAS FEELING	______ ______ ______
WHAT I DID	______ ______ ______

1. In looking back at your recent and past sex offenses, which situations, thoughts, feelings, and behaviors are the same and which are different?

______

______

______

______

2. Are your situations and reactions different enough that you need to complete more than one offense chain?

   ❐ Yes

   ❐ No

Step 7: Sex Offense

In the next step in the chain, everything that has happened before—your goals, strategies, reactions, behavior, what you were thinking and feeling—resulted in you committing a sex offense. The time it takes to move from Step 1 to Step 7 is different for everyone. Moving through those steps can happen very quickly or can take a long time. For some people, all of these steps can happen in an hour. For other people, these steps can take days or weeks or sometimes even months. When you describe your offending in this section, it is important to be specific and honest. It is also important to think about and understand how your own personal history (from chapter 5) and your thoughts, feelings, distortions, and schemas all contributed to your offending.

It is also important to think about the goals you had when you were offending and whether those goals were the same or different from earlier goals. As you may have discovered, what sometimes happens is that, at this point in the offense chain, some people give up on their goals. For example, you may not have wanted to offend, and you may have even tried to prevent an offense earlier in your chain. But, at this point, since your strategies have not worked, you give up your goal and focus more or focus only on what is happening in the immediate situation. Perhaps the steps in the chain were all working toward meeting your goal, up until now, and you were close to meeting your goals.

In the next exercise, you will be asked to describe your sex offense, and to write the details of what happened, what you were thinking, what you were feeling, and what you did. It is important to be very specific for this exercise. Use extra paper if you need to. If you have committed different types of offenses, you will need to do this exercise for each of the ones that are different.

Exercise 6.5
My Sexual Offenses

Start with your most recent offense and describe everything below. Use the extra sheets for other, different types of offenses. You do not need to describe every offense you have ever committed. You can describe many offenses at one time if they were the same or almost the same. What you want to do is look for patterns—things that are similar and things that are different.

Try to answer these questions when you are writing about your offenses:

1. What were your goals while you were offending?
2. How were these goals the same or different from your goals earlier in the offense chain?
3. How was offending an opportunity for you to meet your goals? Which ones? Remember that these can be life goals or goals specifically related to offending.
4. Did you give up on any of your early goals when you were offending? For example, if you did not want to offend earlier in the chain, did you give up on this goal in this situation?
5. What cognitive schemas and distortions played a role in the situation? How did these affect what you did in the situation?
6. Did you feel in control or out of control in the situation? Why or why not?
7. What were your thoughts and feelings in the situation? Please be specific.
8. What were your plans in the situation?

My Most Recent Sex Offense:

My Prior Sex Offense #1:

My Prior Sex Offense #2:

My Prior Sex Offense #3:

1. In looking back at your recent and past sex offenses, which offenses are the same and which are different? In what ways were they the same and in what ways were they different?

____

____

____

____

____

____

____

____

2. Are your offenses different enough that you need to complete more than one offense chain?

   ❒ Yes

   ❒ No

Step 8: What Happens After Offending

What happens after offending is as important as what happens before and during offending because what happens after you do something affects what you will do in the future. If your behavior is rewarded—that is, you feel good or feel that good things have happened—you will be more likely to repeat your actions. If things feel bad—that is, you do not feel good or the situation does not help you to meet your goals—then you will be less likely to repeat your actions. But, this situation can be complicated because after offending you may feel both good and bad, or you may have met some of your goals but not others.

In this section, think about how you felt after you offended. You may have felt bad, felt good, or felt a combination of both. For example, you may have felt sexually satisfied but also bad because you hurt someone and were afraid of being caught, all at the same time. It is important to remember exactly how you felt and what you thought right after offending.

Step 9: Future Plans After Offending

In addition to what happened right after you committed your sex offense, you also thought about and decided what you would do the next time in a similar situation. Some people decide that offending wasn't worth it, that someone was hurt, and they feel bad or guilty or worried about being caught. These people often decide that they will try to not offend again. Sometimes they go back to their goal to prevent offending. Other people feel like they have met their goals, and they decide that the situation was okay, so they determine they will do the same thing again. Some people feel a mixture of both.

In the next exercise, when you are thinking about your reactions right after offending (Step 8), you will be asked to also think about what your future ideas or plans were (Step 9). You may not have actively planned for the future, but it could be that offending met your goals in enough ways that you decided that what you did was a good way to meet your goals. So, in the same situation in the future, you would choose to do the same thing, especially if you knew you wouldn't be caught.

Exercise 6.6: How I Felt After Offending

To understand how you felt after offending—that is, *right after you offended* and not after you were caught—answer these questions:

1. How did you feel right after the offense? What did you feel were some good things about the offense? What did you feel were some not-so-good things? What was the number one reason you would have considered doing it again? What was the number one reason you would have considered not doing it again?

   ____

   ____

   ____

   ____

   ____

   ____

   ____

   ____

2. How did you feel about yourself right after the offense happened? What did this offense say about you? How did you cope with that?

   ____

   ____

   ____

3. How did you feel about the victim right after the offense happened? What did you say to yourself about the victim?

4. Right after offending, did you feel like you had met your goal or goals? Which goals? How were your goals met or not met?

5. What thoughts/feelings do you have now when you think about your offenses?

6. What did you learn from your offenses?

7. Thinking back to your offenses, what would you do differently?

8. Thinking back to your offenses, what were your plans after the offense? What were your plans immediately after the offense? What were your plans a few hours afterward? A few days later?

9. How were these plans related to your good life plan at the time?

10. Did you think you would commit an offense again? Why or why not?

Exercise 6.7: My Offense Chain

Now that you have worked through all of the steps in the offense chain, use the diagram below to put everything together. If you committed different types of sex offenses, you will need to do more than one diagram.

Step 1: Early Life Event

____

____

____

↓

Step 2: My Reaction to Life Event

____

____

____

____

↓

Step 3: My Goals: What I Wanted in the Situation

____

____

____

↓

Step 4: My Strategies: What I Did to Meet My Goals

____

____

____

↓

Step 5: Situation Right Before Offending: Opportunities, High-Risk Situation

Step 6: Behavior: What I Did and Thought Right Before Offending

Step 7: Describe My Sexual Offense

Continued on next page

Step 8: What Happened After I Offended: How Did I Feel? What Did I Think?

____

____

____

↓

Step 9: My Future Plans: What Should or Will I Do Next Time?

____

____

____

____

____

____

Summary

In this section, you have reviewed the nine-step offense chain in detail and have applied it to your own history of offending. We hope these exercises have helped you to develop a much better understanding of exactly what happened so you can have a better future and can prevent yourself from offending again. If you have completed these exercises correctly, you have almost certainly worked very hard. We hope you have kept in mind that, although it is natural to feel bad about your actions, it is not helpful to you or to others if you feel bad about who you are. In fact, if you have given these exercises your best effort, that fact alone says a lot about your commitment to a better future.

In the next part of this workbook, you will take the knowledge you have gained about yourself and will explore specific pathways to offending, which relate to the goals and strategies involved in the offense chain.

CHAPTER 7

Pathways to Offending

In the previous chapter of this workbook, you described in detail the steps in your offense chain. You may have prepared more than one offense chain because you have committed different types of offenses. Also, in chapter 3, you looked at your self-regulation style. In this next section, you will look again at self-regulation and will analyze what was happening during your path or paths to offending.

There are four pathways to offending, based on your *offense goals* during the offense chain (Step 3) and the *strategies* you used to meet these goals (Step 4). Your therapist will help you determine your offense pathway based on your assessments and on the work you do in this chapter as well as the work you did in chapter 6. The information you gain from treatment and these exercises may also be used to refine your assessments.

Offense-Related Goals

The first part of determining your offense pathway is to look back at your goals during Step 2 of the offense chain. Recall the two types of goals:

Avoidance Goals: You have an avoidance goal when you don't want something to happen, such as when you want to prevent yourself from offending or when you don't want to harm someone by abuse.

Approach Goals: You have an approach goal when you want something to happen and are looking forward to it or are working toward it. The goal may not be specific to sex or sexual offending or aggression, but it leads to offending later in the chain. It is important to note that these goals are different from the positive approach goals in your good life plan (from chapter 2). Although you may find some overlap in the two types of goals, the approach goals described here relate specifically to your offense chain.

Consider the following example:

Dominic is a young man of 21. He just entered a new treatment program. When he was 15, he bribed his sister to have sex. He would pin her down, all the while telling himself that she would enjoy the experience as it progressed. In fact, his sister went to her teacher, who called the police. Dominic went to a residential program where he didn't do well. He was discharged when he turned 18 years old, and returned to live with his mother. He recently committed another offense when his sister visited. During her visit, Dominic was aware that her intentions were not sexual, but he began to experience sexual arousal toward her again. At first, he tried to ignore the feelings, but the more he tried not to think about them, the more aroused he got. He began to think if he initiated sex, his sister might consent, as she had seemed to in the past. He told himself that if she actively said, "No," he would stop. As his impulsive attempts to initiate sex progressed, however, he became increasingly aroused and could not cope with the fact that his sister did not want to comply. She became clearly distressed, but by this point, Dominic was focused only on having sex and raped her. In recounting this offense, Dominic expressed confusion and self-hatred. He said he had known better at the time, and yet having sex with his sister had not seemed like such a bad idea in the moment.

In this example, Dominic wanted to avoid offending but he did not do anything to meet his goal other than to try not to think about it. He had little ability to control his urges or to avoid re-offending. He was aroused and focused on sexual behavior and was unable to think about anything else at that moment. Dominic's offense-related goal was an *avoidant* goal.

Here is another example:

Ken had long felt bad about his sexual orientation. As a deeply religious person, he spent much of his life trying to tell himself that he had no sexual interest in males. Ken became involved with a small church in his neighborhood. He hoped that his church activities would distract him from his attraction to young men. The other people his age at the church seemed distant, and Ken grew increasingly lonely. He found himself still attracted to young men in the area, and felt he had no one he could talk with openly. Feeling very lonely, he made contact with several young men. He told himself that he would not offend against them and that they could benefit from the wisdom he had accrued through years of his devout faith. When he had a discussion with a 15-year-old male about homosexuality, however, Ken found it hard to stay focused on religion. Ken could tell that the young man wasn't sure about his own sexuality. Despite Ken's better judgment, he quickly said things that led to sexual activity with the young man. Afterward, Ken felt very depressed and told himself he was no good.

Ken's goal was to avoid offending. He was uncomfortable with his attraction to males, and knew he was in a position of authority because he was much older than the young man. Part of the reason Ken was so involved with his church was to keep focused on religion rather than his interest in young males. Ken's offense-related goal was *avoidant*.

Here is a third example:

Jay grew up in a home where his father was a drug dealer who abused his mother. Jay often went to live with relatives and in foster homes when his parents were in trouble with the law. Jay developed few emotional connections to others and came to view the world as a place where one has to have fun when opportunities arise. He also came to believe that most authority figures were hostile, controlling, and unpredictable.

Jay eventually went to a juvenile detention center where he forced sex onto younger teens when the staff wasn't looking. Jay did not actively plan his assaults during these times. Instead, he saw the opportunities when they presented themselves and would say later that, "Something just came over me." Others regarded Jay as a "tough guy" and looked up to him, which made him feel superior and worthwhile. His attitude toward these assaults was that the behavior itself was fun and worth the risk.

After he left the detention center, Jay sexually assaulted a woman in the bathroom of a local bar. Jay believed that women in general could not be trusted to tell the truth, particularly in sexual matters. He thought that this woman had flirted with him, which, in his mind, justified the assault. In Jay's view, the woman "owed" him. He had actually not had any particular plans to assault anyone that evening. Jay felt positive about his actions that evening, because he had gotten sex. To others, this assault seemed to come from "out of the blue."

Jay has an approach goal for offending. Throughout his life, he has focused on getting pleasure and having good times when he wants them. It has always been easy for Jay to notice opportunities to get what he wants, and when that happens, he always moves quickly. Jay's offense-related goal in the bar was an *approach* goal.

Here is one last example:

Miguel had recently moved into a new house across from a single-parent family. Miguel noticed that an eight-year-old boy, Timmy, lived in the other house. Miguel wondered what it would be like to spend time with the boy. Would Timmy be okay with playing sex games, Miguel wondered? Timmy's mother was working hard to make ends meet, and Miguel introduced himself to her. He offered to do favors for her, such as yard work. He made up his mind that he would like to spend time with Timmy and so he came up with ways to be helpful to the child's mother, so that he could be around Timmy. Miguel was enjoying the process of getting to know the two of them, but he particularly enjoyed the anticipation of getting to spend time alone with Timmy. Miguel hoped that his efforts would result in sex, but he also knew that he needed to behave innocently in case the mother noticed that he was sexually interested in Timmy. Miguel worked to appear helpful and innocent. He was anticipating that this could be good for Timmy, as well. One day, Miguel offered to look after Timmy so that his mother could get some time alone with her friends. During that time, he sexually assaulted Timmy.

Miguel clearly has an *approach goal* with respect to offending. He anticipated offending and worked to minimize the risks to himself. He made and carried out specific plans in order to form a relationship with both Timmy and his mother. His initial desire (Step 2) and his goal (Step 3) were to build a relationship with Timmy so that he could gain sexual access to him. He experienced positive emotions about offending as he waited for an opportunity, and he looked forward to offending against Timmy.

Exercise 7.1:
My Goals in the Offense Chain

For this exercise, first look back at steps 2 and 3 in your own offense chain from exercise 6.3. Think about your goals during those steps in your offense chain and answer the following questions. If you need to do this exercise several times, for more than one offense, please use additional paper for your answers.

1. When did you first notice the urge or desire to act out sexually? If your desire at first was not for sex but was for something else, such as intimacy or a chance to express anger, at what point did you first notice the sexual desire?

____

____

____

____

2. What was that like for you?

____

____

____

____

3. Think about your thoughts and emotions at that time. Were you afraid or fearful that you would act on your desires? Or were you looking forward to the situation being positive for you?

____

____

____

____

4. What did you do when you noticed the sexual urge or desire?

____

____

____

____

5. What were you hoping would happen?

____

____

____

____

6. Were you concerned or afraid that something bad would happen if you followed through with your sexual urges (e.g., someone would get hurt, you'd be caught)? What specific things were you concerned about?

____

____

____

____

7. Were you thinking that something good would happen if you acted on your urges? Even if you were afraid that something bad might happen, were you also looking forward to something? If so, what was it?

____

____

____

____

8. Thinking back over your other offenses, whether or not you have been convicted for them, which of your reactions at the time were similar, and which were different?

____

____

____

____

9. Looking back at your answers to these questions, would you say your offense-related goal was an avoidance goal or an approach goal?

   ❒ Avoidance Goal
   ❒ Approach Goal

   Please explain your choice:

____

____

____

____

Offense-Related Strategies

As explained above, offense pathways are a combination of the offense-related goals and the strategies used to meet these goals. Recall that strategies can be passive or active.

Passive Strategies: When you use passive strategies, you don't really plan your behavior or your reactions, or you may just try to ignore what is happening. Passive strategies also are the ones you use when you respond impulsively or without thinking, or when you react quickly to things that are going on around you, based on your beliefs and schemas.

Active Strategies: When your strategies are active, you plan your behavior so you can meet your offense-related goal. Planning can vary from just a little bit of planning to very complex and detailed planning. The key with active strategies is that the person does *something* to meet his goal, whether or not this works out in the end.

Before looking at your own strategies, let's return to the earlier examples and consider their goals and strategies:

Dominic had an avoidance goal at the time of his last offense. He wanted to avoid offending, but he didn't have the skills he needed to prevent himself from offending. Dominic's strategies were passive because he mostly just tried to ignore his thoughts and urges. Dominic did not do anything to meet his goal of avoiding offending other than to try not to think about it. However, he was sexually aroused and had a very hard time thinking of anything else. Dominic's general strategy for managing problem situations is to avoid them or to try not to think about them. Dominic's strategies were *passive.*

Ken also wanted to avoid offending. Ken actively tried to do things so that he wouldn't offend, even though these strategies didn't work. He tried reminding himself not to offend and tried to stop himself when he was having thoughts about offending. He also tried to focus on religious activities as a way of avoiding offending. His attempts to avoid his interest in teenage boys by being a mentor to them not only failed, but made it more likely he would offend. As a result, his attempts to avoid offending failed quickly. Ken's strategies were *active* even though they did not work.

Jay had an approach goal to offending, and his strategies were largely passive and automatic. He didn't plan his offending—or his reactions to other situations—but he was quick to act when the right opportunity presented itself. Jay's response to opportunities to offend was automatic. Jay did not always actively plan out his offenses in advance. Instead, whenever opportunities to offend arose, he took advantage of them. Jay's strategies were *passive* and *automatic.*

In the last example, Miguel had an approach goal of having sex with Timmy, and he engaged in planning and behavior that explicitly increased the chance of having access to Timmy, such as befriending Timmy's mother. Miguel's strategies included being helpful to the mother, doing work for her, and offering to baby-sit. Miguel was also aware that Timmy's mother needed all the help she could get, and he used this situation to his advantage. Miguel's strategies were *explicit.* Miguel took active steps to sexually offend. He worked to create situations where he could gain access to Timmy, moving carefully one step at a time. Miguel's strategies were *active* and *explicit.*

Exercise 7.2: My Strategies in the Offense Chain

Now, look back at your answers for Step 4 in your own offense chain (exercise 6.3). In that exercise, you looked at the strategies you used to meet your goals. In this next exercise, you will focus only on your offense strategies at that step. If you need to do this exercise several times, for more than one offense, please use additional paper for your answers.

Answer the following questions:

1. How did you meet or encounter the victim of your offense?

   ____

   ____

   ____

2. How long was it after the first time you saw the victim that you thought about having sex with him or her?

   ____

   ____

   ____

3. After first experiencing the desire, how long was it before you approached someone for sex or to meet other goals?

   ____

   ____

   ____

4. How quickly or spontaneously did the offense seem to happen? Please describe.

   ____

   ____

   ____

5. How in or out of control overall did you feel in the situation?

   ____

   ____

   ____

6. How in or out of control of your thoughts did you feel in the situation?

___

___

7. How in or out of control of your emotions did you feel in the situation?

___

___

___

8. How in or out of control of your behavior did you feel in the situation?

___

___

___

9. How in or out of control of your sexual urges did you feel in the situation?

___

___

___

10. How impulsively did you choose your strategies? In other words, were your strategies planned or in reaction to the situation?

___

___

___

11. Thinking back on your offense(s), please describe the extent of your planning prior to the offense(s).

___

___

___

12. How did you deal with the emotions you experienced during your offense chain?

___

___

___

13. Describe the ways you may have felt overwhelmed or like you did not know what to do in the situation. Or, if you felt in control, describe what you did.

___

___

___

14. What things, if any, did you try to do to control your urges or to stop the situation or to stop yourself from offending?

___

___

___

15. Thinking back over other offenses and similar situations, whether you have been convicted for these or not, which of your reactions were similar and which were different?

___

___

___

16. Looking back at your answers to these questions, were your strategies passive or active?

❒ Passive ❒ Automatic

❒ Active ❒ Explicit

Please explain your choice.

___

___

___

___

___

Defining Offense Pathways

As you can see from the exercises you completed above, goals and strategies are different for everyone and sometimes for the same person, depending on the specific situation. Different people follow different pathways. Sometimes the same person follows the same pathway for all offenses he has committed, while other people follow different pathways for different offenses. As you consider the exercises and the definitions below, be sure to discuss and confirm your thoughts about your pathway(s) with your therapist, who also will be thinking about your pathway(s) and working with you on this in treatment. Remember, you should do these exercises based on all offense situations you have been in, whether you were convicted for them or not. The four offense pathways are as follows:

Avoidant-Passive Pathway: This pathway happens when the person's goal is to avoid offending, but he does not do anything to meet this goal—that is, he doesn't use any strategies. Sometimes, he really just doesn't know what to do in the situation, so he doesn't do anything. He may try to ignore the situation or ignore his desires and urges or he may even deny that he is feeling anything or that he is at risk. Offending happens later in this offense chain because this person did not take action to stop his offense progression. In the middle of the offense chain, he gives up on his goal of avoiding an offense and instead approaches it. After offending, he may have negative emotions and see the offense as a negative experience. He may, in fact, resolve to himself or others to not offend again, but because he does not know what to do to meet this goal, he often ends up offending again. In the examples provided above, Dominic is an example of a person who has an *avoidant-passive pathway.* His goal was avoidant and his strategies to try to meet this goal were passive.

Avoidant-Active Pathway: This pathway happens when the person's goal is to avoid offending. He tries to meet his goal by using strategies to gain control or to stop his thoughts or his behavior. But the strategies he uses are not effective, and they actually increase his risk to offend. For example, he may use alcohol, drugs, or pornography to control his urges or mood, but those strategies just increase his urges. Offending happens later in the offense chain because his strategies to avoid offending were not effective. Later in the offense chain, he gives up on his goal to avoid offending and then chooses instead to approach it. After offending, he may have negative emotions and see the offense as a negative experience. He may, in fact, resolve to himself and to others that he will not offend again. But because he does not have strategies in place that work, he often ends up offending again. In the above examples, Ken is an example of a person with an *avoidant-active pathway.* His goal was to avoid offending, and his strategies were active (but unsuccessful for preventing offending).

Approach-Automatic Pathway: This pathway occurs when a person's goal moves him toward offending: He has an approach goal. He may, at the time, even be moving toward a life goal, but the pursuit of his life goal later results in an offense. This person may be impulsive or may see opportunities to meet life or offense-related goals in situations as they come up—that is, he reacts to what is going on around him, and filters the situation through his schemas. As the offense chain unfolds and he sees he is meeting his goal, he continues toward his goal until he commits an offense. After the offense, he feels it is a positive experience because he has met his goals. Both the reinforcement he gets for meeting his goals and the fact that the offense is a positive experience for him increase his risk to offend again. The fact that his attitudes and schemas are that offending is okay also increases his risk. In the examples above, Jay is an example of a person with an *approach-automatic pathway.* He had an approach goal regarding offending and his strategies were passive and automatic because he reacted quickly to what was going on around him.

Approach-Explicit Pathway: This pathway happens when a person's goal moves him toward offending. In this situation, the person has an approach goal. He may, at the time, think he is moving toward a life goal, but this is also an offense-related goal and results in offending. His strategies to meet his goals are very well planned and his schemas are those that make him think that offending is an okay way to meet his goals. As his offense chain unfolds and his strategies and planning are successful, he continues until he commits an offense. After the offense, he feels it is a positive experience because he has met his goals. The reinforcement he gets for meeting his goals and the fact that the offense is a positive experience for him increase his risk to offend again. The fact that his attitudes and schemas both say that offending is okay also increases his risk. In the examples above, Miguel is an example of a person with an *approach-explicit pathway.* He has an approach goal regarding offending, and he intentionally uses active strategies to make offenses happen.

Exercise 7.3:
My Offense Pathway

Recall from what you read above that an offense pathway is a combination of your offense goals and the strategies you use to meet these goals. Your next step in understanding your own pathway is to put your goals and strategies together to determine exactly what kind of offense pathway you followed in offending. Your offense pathway can give you a lot of information that tells you what happens and also how you tend to respond. Understanding your pathway gives you a better understanding of exactly what happens when you commit offenses. Importantly, it also helps you and your therapist to understand what you should do in treatment and what skills you need to learn and practice, both during treatment and afterward.

Below you will find a chart.

1. For determining your own offense pathway, review your answers about your goals and strategies and then determine your pathway, using the chart below. Fill in the following chart based on your *most recent offense(s).* First, place a circle around your offense goal. Second, place a circle around your offense strategy. Last, find the box that corresponds to both of these together, and color in or circle this box.

		STRATEGY	
		Passive	Active
GOAL	Avoidant	Avoidant-Passive	Avoidant-Active
	Approach	Approach-Automatic	Approach-Explicit

2. What does this information tell you about your offense pathway and your patterns?

____

____

____

____

Sometimes, a person follows the same pathway for every single offense he commits, while other people follow different pathways for different offenses they have committed. This difference in pathways is very important for you to consider. You may have been in treatment programs where you were taught about only one "cycle" of abuse. Part of that treatment would then involve working out how the cycle of abuse applied to you. Professionals increasingly have realized, however, that individuals follow many different pathways to offending. So in this workbook we never assume that all people follow the same cycle of abuse. People follow many different pathways to offending, either over time or for different types of offenses. For example, people who have offended multiple times may have started out with one pathway, such as the avoidant-active pathway, but later, over time, have adopted a more approach-explicit pathway in their behavior. Other people may follow one pathway during their offenses against children, but a different pathway for their offenses against adults.

Think back to all of your offenses and determine your offense goals, strategies, and pathways. As you start to develop your skills to manage your risk and to implement your good life plan, it will be important for you to know if you tend to follow different pathways at different times. If your pathways were different for any reason, complete the chart below as many times as you need to for all offenses that had different patterns. You can fill in this chart up to four times.

Remember, this exercise applies not only to situations where you were convicted, but to other situations where you committed an offense but weren't caught or charged. You don't need to describe each offense separately. Instead, look at the situations that were similar for each type of pathway so you can understand how your behavior developed and changed over time and across situations. Remember, the process you are going through is to help you to understand your individual patterns.

3. If you have a second pathway, circle your goals, strategies, and pathway here:

		STRATEGY	
		Passive	Active
GOAL	Avoidant	Avoidant-Passive	Avoidant-Active
	Approach	Approach-Automatic	Approach-Explicit

4. What offense(s) do/does this pathway apply to?

5. If you have a third pathway, circle your goals, strategies, and pathway here:

		STRATEGY	
		Passive	Active
GOAL	Avoidant	Avoidant-Passive	Avoidant-Active
	Approach	Approach-Automatic	Approach-Explicit

6. What offense(s) do/does this pathway apply to?

____

____

____

____

7. If you have a fourth pathway, circle your goals, strategies, and pathway here:

		STRATEGY	
		Passive	Active
GOAL	Avoidant	Avoidant-Passive	Avoidant-Active
	Approach	Approach-Automatic	Approach-Explicit

8. What offense(s) do/does this pathway apply to?

____

____

____

____

9. Looking back over your different pathways, what have you learned about your patterns? What is similar about your offenses or your behavior, and what is different?

____

____

____

____

10. What changes do you see over time?

____

____

____

____

11. How can you use this information in treatment to make changes and to prevent offending again?

____

____

____

____

____

____

____

____

Summary

In this section you have explored your pathways to your sexual offenses. This process involves understanding your goals and strategies as well as the different features of each pathway. In the next part of this workbook, you will examine your life in greater detail, explore who you want to be in the future, and begin the process of developing your future good life plan.

CHAPTER 8

Who Am I and Who Can I Be?

Now that you have come to an understanding of your common life goals, the risk factors that have contributed to your offense(s), your offense chain, and your personal history, this part of the workbook focuses on putting those pieces together into a more complete understanding of who you are and who you can be.

In chapter 5, you worked on who you were as a child, teenager, and young adult in order to understand your good life plans at those times. This chapter is designed to help you start looking at who you want to be in the future. It is also designed to help you understand how you need to manage things like your motivation and risk factors when you develop your risk management plan and good life plan, which you will do in chapters 10 and 11.

Exercise 8.1: My Motivation Now

First, go back to exercises 1.1, 1.2, and 1.3 in chapter 1 of this workbook. Recall that these exercises explored the importance of making changes to your life and looked at your confidence in making those changes. Those exercises also focused on your internal *desire*, *ability*, *reason*, and *need* for making changes to your life. The purpose of this next exercise is to explore your motivation to change now that you are farther along in a course of changing your life and meeting your life goals.

1. As you look at your previous answers, how would your answers be different now?

____

____

____

____

____

2. How has your motivation for change grown and developed since you completed chapter 1 of this workbook?

____

____

____

____

____

3. What do your answers in chapter 1 say about you? What do they say about who you can be?

____

____

____

____

____

4. What areas remain for you to work on? What are your plans and strategies to keep your motivation as you move forward?

____

____

____

____

____

____

You can use your answers to these questions to reflect further on who you are and who you can be, as you continue to explore changes you can make to your life.

Exercise 8.2: My Common Life Goals, Then and Now

Now, go back to your answers in exercise 2.1, in chapter 2, about common life goals and review how these goals have been important to you in the past and how they are important to you now. Here is the overview of them again:

Chart 1: Common Life Goals

COMMON LIFE GOALS	
Life: Living and Surviving	This goal is important to people who think about or spend time being healthy or making sure they are able to meet their basic needs. Positive ways to meet this goal: - Exercising - Eating well - Taking care of their physical health - Surviving in the world, staying alive and safe Negative ways to meet this goal: - Spending time looking out for threats to their well-being or safety - Being hostile toward others seen as threatening
Knowledge: Learning and Knowing	This goal is important to people who think about or spend time seeking knowledge or information. Positive ways to meet this goal: - Going to school, completing training, taking courses - Learning about themselves, such as in treatment - Mentoring others Negative ways to meet this goal: - Teaching children about sex
Being Good at Work and Play	This goal is important to people who think about or spend time trying to be good at work or leisure activities. Positive ways to meet this goal: - Being good at sports or hobbies - Being good at a job - Getting education or training to become better at a job

Continued on next page

COMMON LIFE GOALS	
Personal Choice and Independence	This goal is important to people who think about or spend time being independent and making their own way in life. Positive ways to meet this goal: * Valuing personal choice in most situations * Making plans to meet a goal * Being assertive Negative ways to meet this goal: * Controlling, dominating, or abusing others * Feeling that the world is a dangerous place, or that they have to "get" others before they get them
Peace of Mind	This goal is important to people who think about or spend time trying to be calm and relaxed, or trying to reduce stress and its effects in their lives. Positive ways to meet this goal: * Trying to reduce emotional distress or stress * Exercising or meditating to relax or stay calm * Trying not to be impulsive or angry Negative ways to meet this goal: * Using alcohol, drugs, or medication to relax or to cope with emotions * Using sex or masturbation to relax or to cope with emotions * Having sexual relationships, even with people who cannot truly consent
Relationships and Friendships	This goal is important to people who think about or spend time with family, friends, or romantic partners. Positive ways to meet this goal: * Spending time with family * Spending time with friends * Wanting or having an intimate/sexual relationship * Supporting family, friends, or a partner Negative ways to meet this goal: * Being a member of a gang

COMMON LIFE GOALS	
Community: Being Part of a Group	This goal is important to people who think about or spend time being a part of a specific group of people. Positive ways to meet this goal: * Being or wanting to be part of a group with those that have things in common, such as a Lion's Club or the military * Doing volunteer work * Being part of their neighborhood * Feeling that a group is important Negative ways to meet this goal: * Being a member of a gang * Being a member of a man/boy love club
Spirituality: Having Meaning in Life	This goal is important to people who think about or spend time looking for a purpose or meaning in life. Positive ways to meet this goal: * Participating in religious or spiritual activities (e.g., church, sweat lodge) * Meditation or praying * Reading or studying spiritual materials (e.g., the Bible)
Happiness	This goal is important to people who think about or spend time wanting to be content or happy, or to experience pleasure. Positive ways to meet this goal: * Doing things that give them a sense of satisfaction or fulfillment * Doing things that give them a sense of pleasure (e.g., sex) * Doing things to get a sense of purpose or direction in life (e.g., work, friendships, family) * Participating in treatment Negative ways to meet this goal: * Pleasurable but illegal activities, such as drug abuse or sexual abuse

Continued on next page

COMMON LIFE GOALS	
Creativity	This goal is important to people who think about or spend time creating or trying new things or looking for excitement. Positive ways to meet this goal: * Trying new things they have not done before * Painting, building things, drawing, etc. Negative ways to meet this goal: * Trying newer types of sex or more exciting sex

1. Next, write down which of these goals is important, very important, and extremely important to you as you look toward the next five years of your life.

   My **important** goals are:

   ____

   ____

   ____

   ____

   ____

   My **very important** goals are:

   ____

   ____

   ____

   ____

   ____

   My **extremely important** goals are:

   ____

   ____

   ____

   ____

   ____

Exercise 8.3: Approach Versus Avoidance Goals

Remember that in chapter 3 you learned about *approach* and *avoidance goals*. For example, an approach goal would be setting a goal of staying calm in stressful situations (this state of calmness is something you are working toward), while an avoidance goal would be setting a goal of not letting things make you angry (being angry is something you hope will not happen and that you want to avoid).

1. Take some time and think about the positive approach goals you have tried to achieve or you have had in the past:

____

____

____

____

____

2. What are some positive, good life *approach goals* you have in your life now?

____

____

____

____

____

3. What are some of the *positive avoidance goals* you've had in the past (for example, not offending, staying out of trouble)?

____

____

____

____

____

____

4. What are some good life *avoidance goals* you have now?

5. What are some ways you can look at your positive avoidance goals differently? What are some ways you could turn them into approach goals? For example, "not forcing someone to have sex" is a positive avoidance goal. At the same time, you could also have the positive approach goal of "a fulfilling and healthy sex life that is not harmful to anyone." "Staying out of trouble" can also be the positive goal of "living a balanced and self-determined life-style." Take some time and write your thoughts below:

6. What do your answers say about the progress you are making?

7. What do your answers say about you? What do they say about who you can be?

8. What is left for you to do in this area?

Exercise 8.4: Problems Meeting My Goals

Next, please review your answers to the questions in exercise 2.3 (chapter 2) about the problems or flaws that may have existed in your attempts to meet these common life goals. Here are examples of some of the possible flaws:

Chart 2: Common Problems Meeting Goals

FLAWS (PROBLEMS)	WHAT HAPPENS WHEN PEOPLE HAVE THIS PROBLEM	EXAMPLES
Ways to Meet Goals (Means)	This problem is about the ways people try to meet their goals—what they actually do that doesn't work or that causes problems.	• Being jealous or trying to control your partner to get intimacy or sex, but behaving in a way that pushes your partner away. • Getting arrested because you had sex with a child when what you really wanted was a relationship with an adult, but you didn't or couldn't figure out how to have one. • Stealing to get money to survive, but you end up in jail with no money. • Using sex or masturbation to cope with emotions like anger, but the relief only lasts only a short time and your anger returns.
Too Narrow a Good Life Plan (Scope)	This problem happens when people don't have enough goals in their lives—when they rely on only one or two things to make them happy or to allow them to feel good. They have a few things that are important to them in their lives, but those things are not enough. A good life plan that is too narrow often focuses on short-term happiness rather than long-term fulfillment and sustained happiness.	• The only thing that is important or the most important thing to you is sex or partying. • The most important thing is your wife or husband, but then your partner leaves you. • Wanting a good job, but being unwilling or unable to get the necessary education or training for it.

FLAWS (PROBLEMS)	WHAT HAPPENS WHEN PEOPLE HAVE THIS PROBLEM	EXAMPLES
Conflict Between Goals	This problem happens when people's different goals in life don't match up, or when meeting one goal means that they then can't meet another goal.	* Wanting a relationship with one person, but also wanting sexual freedom with other people. * Wanting to make money to support your family, but not wanting or being able to work. * Wanting to spend time with your friends but also wanting to hold a job (for example, staying out late the night before and not being able to do your job the next day).
Lack of Skills	This problem happens when people don't have the skills or strategies to do what they want in life to meet their goals.	* Wanting to get a good job, but not finishing school and so being unable to get the job. * Wanting to have a long-term relationship, but not knowing how to meet people or how to keep a relationship. * Wanting happiness and pleasure, but not knowing how to get those things except through illegal or unhealthy behavior, such as drugs and alcohol.
Lack of Opportunities	This problem happens when people don't have the opportunities to meet their goals because external factors beyond their control prevent them from meeting the goal.	* Wanting to be with your family, but not being allowed to because of parole or probation conditions. * Wanting to get a certain job, but finding that no one will hire you. * Wanting a better job, but not being able to get the training or education you need.

1. As you review exercise 2.3, ask yourself how your answers would be different now?

____

____

____

____

____

2. How has your understanding of flaws and your ability to manage them grown and developed?

____

____

____

____

____

3. Use the chart below to write which specific strategies you have learned to use, so that you can deal with each flaw or problem you face?

FLAW	MY STRATEGIES
Ways to Meet Goals (Means)	1. ________________ ________________ 2. ________________ ________________ 3. ________________ ________________ 4. ________________ ________________ 5. ________________ ________________

FLAW	MY STRATEGIES
Too Narrow a Good Life Plan (Scope)	1. __________ __________ 2. __________ __________ 3. __________ __________ 4. __________ __________ 5. __________ __________
Conflict Between Goals	1. __________ __________ 2. __________ __________ 3. __________ __________ 4. __________ __________ 5. __________ __________

FLAW	MY STRATEGIES
Lack of Skills	1. ______________________________ ______________________________ 2. ______________________________ ______________________________ 3. ______________________________ ______________________________ 4. ______________________________ ______________________________ 5. ______________________________ ______________________________
Lack of Opportunities	1. ______________________________ ______________________________ 2. ______________________________ ______________________________ 3. ______________________________ ______________________________ 4. ______________________________ ______________________________ 5. ______________________________ ______________________________

4. What work remains for you to do to develop the needed strategies for tackling each of these flaws?

____

____

____

____

____

5. What do your answers say about you? What do they say about who you can be?

____

____

____

____

____

You can use your answers to reflect further on how you can better manage these flaws in the future.

Exercise 8.5: My Risk Factors

Recall that in the self-examination exercise in chapter 4, you outlined which risk factors you felt were important in your offending and in your life in general. You also discussed which risk factors other people felt contributed to your sexual offending.

1. Review your answers to the self-examination exercise. Ask yourself what you've learned about how you will manage these risk factors over the coming months and years.

____

____

____

____

____

2. How has your understanding of risk factors and your ability to manage them changed and grown?

____

____

____

____

____

3. What specific risk management strategies have you developed for your risk factors? In the chart below, first write each of your risk factors and then write the strategies you have developed for managing each one.

RISK FACTOR	MY STRATEGIES
#1	1. _______________ _______________ 2. _______________ _______________ 3. _______________ _______________ 4. _______________ _______________ 5. _______________ _______________

RISK FACTOR	MY STRATEGIES
#2	1. ______________________ ______________________ 2. ______________________ ______________________ 3. ______________________ ______________________ 4. ______________________ ______________________ 5. ______________________ ______________________
#3	1. ______________________ ______________________ 2. ______________________ ______________________ 3. ______________________ ______________________ 4. ______________________ ______________________ 5. ______________________ ______________________

Continued on next page

RISK FACTOR	MY STRATEGIES
#4	1. ____________ ____________ 2. ____________ ____________ 3. ____________ ____________ 4. ____________ ____________ 5. ____________ ____________
#5	1. ____________ ____________ 2. ____________ ____________ 3. ____________ ____________ 4. ____________ ____________ 5. ____________ ____________

RISK FACTOR	MY STRATEGIES
#6	1. ________________ ________________ 2. ________________ ________________ 3. ________________ ________________ 4. ________________ ________________ 5. ________________ ________________
#7	1. ________________ ________________ 2. ________________ ________________ 3. ________________ ________________ 4. ________________ ________________ 5. ________________ ________________

Continued on next page

RISK FACTOR	MY STRATEGIES
#8	1. ______ ______ 2. ______ ______ 3. ______ ______ 4. ______ ______ 5. ______ ______
#9	1. ______ ______ 2. ______ ______ 3. ______ ______ 4. ______ ______ 5. ______ ______

RISK FACTOR	MY STRATEGIES
#10	1. ______________________ ______________________ 2. ______________________ ______________________ 3. ______________________ ______________________ 4. ______________________ ______________________ 5. ______________________ ______________________

4. What work is left for you to do so that you can manage your risk factors?

____

____

____

____

____

5. What do your answers say about you? What do they say about who you can be?

____

____

____

____

____

You can use your answers to reflect further on how you can better manage these flaws in the future.

6. Next, go back to exercise 3.1 where you related your schemas to your life. In chapter 4, you also reviewed schemas that contribute to sexual abuse and other crimes. Remember, you identified which of these schemas were most important in your life and offenses. As you review your answers in that earlier exercise, ask yourself how would your answers be different now.

7. How has your understanding of schemas and their influence on your life grown and developed?

8. What do your answers say about you? What do they say about who you can be?

9. What work is left for you to do to manage your schemas?

You can use your answers to reflect further on how you can better manage these flaws in the future.

10. Next, please review what your wrote for your personal history from chapter 5. Having reviewed all of these exercises, what are some of the most important take-away lessons you have drawn from reviewing your life?

____

____

____

____

____

11. How has your understanding of your life grown and developed in the course of going through this workbook and through treatment?

____

____

____

____

____

12. What do your answers say about you? What do they say about who you can be?

____

____

____

____

____

13. What is left for you to do?

____

____

____

____

____

14. As we move closer to the final exercise in this part of the workbook, ask yourself how your schemas and beliefs about sex and sex offending are different now than they were when you first entered treatment.

____

____

____

____

____

15. How has your understanding of these attitudes and beliefs grown and developed?

____

____

____

____

____

16. What do your answers say about you? What do they say about who you can be?

____

____

____

____

____

Before you move to the final exercise in this part of the workbook, carefully reflect on the following questions:

17. How is your ability to use self-regulation in your daily life different now than it was when you entered treatment?

____

____

____

18. How has your understanding of self-regulation grown and developed?

19. What specific skills have you developed to improve your self-regulation?

20. What do your answers say about you? What do they say about who you can be?

21. What skills are left for you to develop so that you can have effective self-regulation?

____

____

____

____

____

22. What skills are left for you to develop so that you can manage your risk to re-offend?

____

____

____

____

____

Now, take some time to review all of your answers, and then write down five things you can do as your next steps to help you develop a balanced and self-directed good life plan. The idea is that you can keep yourself focused on these steps and also track your progress, both on your own and with the other people in your life. You may find that it helps to get together with others who have done this exercise, and review your progress and successes on a regular basis. Research has shown that reviewing positive progress helps build more success.

My Next Steps

1. _______________
2. _______________
3. _______________
4. _______________
5. _______________

Lastly, having reviewed all of these exercises and the life summary you have just written, you can write a "Who I Can Be" summary below. It can contain the following:

- The common life goals most important to you
- The most important ways you can achieve those goals
- The most important problems you expect you will have in achieving your life goals
- The most important risk factors for offending and how you can manage those risk factors in the future
- The most important attitudes and beliefs that can influence your actions in a positive direction
- The strengths you have and how you can use these to keep moving forward
- How you can move forward to having a good life without offending

Who I Can Be

Continued on next page

Summary

Congratulations on completing a series of very difficult exercises! It is our hope that you have found these explorations of your life and your future helpful. The next parts of this workbook focus on change in treatment, with the development of a good life plan and a look ahead at the future.

CHAPTER 9

Bringing It All Together: Integrating Treatment Change

In this workbook, you have looked at the many different parts of your life that are related to your goals and to your offending. In your treatment program, you will have learned even more about these areas and about what is unique to you. In chapter 8, you looked at building a better understanding of who you are and who you can be. This next part of the workbook will help you bring all of your learning together in preparation for developing your risk management plan in chapter 10 and your good life plan in chapter 11. This part, chapter 9, picks up where the previous parts have left off, except for one thing: We expect that, by this time in treatment, you will have reviewed the earlier parts in detail with your therapist and with other supportive people in your life. You will have addressed other areas with your therapist in your treatment program, as well, that can be important to offending. These areas will depend on your personal circumstances. They may include:

- Cognitive schemas (those not covered in this workbook)
- Cognitive skills (problem-solving, critical thinking, self-monitoring)
- Cognitive distortions
- Managing your emotions
- Managing sexual arousal and abuse-related fantasies
- Intimate and social relationships
- Understanding the impact of sexual offenses on victims
- Making amends to those harmed by sexual offending
- Taking responsibility for your actions

- Mental health and other conditions relevant to living a healthy, satisfying life
- Substance abuse treatment
- Attitudes and beliefs about offending
- Human sexuality
- Opportunities to practice new skills and to get feedback from others

Some of these topics are not directly included in this workbook because this book focuses specifically on common life goals and self-regulation. Also, information and exercises about some of these other topics are already available in other workbooks, and each treatment program addresses these topics differently. Regardless, you should have addressed each of these topics in treatment, as needed. As you complete the exercises in this chapter, and in the rest of the workbook, it will be important to consider all of these different topic areas in order to ensure your plans are complete and that they are set up to allow you to achieve success.

Exercise 9.1: What I Have Learned That I Can Use for My Risk Management Plan and My Good Life Plan

First let's examine what you've learned so far in the following areas. You have probably learned additional information from your therapist and from your treatment program. Write a summary of what you have learned in the following areas.

1. Changing and managing my risk factors:

____

____

____

____

____

____

____

2. Changing my schemas:

3. Changing and challenging my cognitive distortions:

4. Developing problem-solving skills:

5. Managing my emotions:

6. Managing my deviant arousal and fantasies:

____

____

____

____

____

7. Developing my skills for healthy relationships:

____

____

____

____

____

8. Developing my intimacy skills:

____

____

____

____

____

9. Developing supportive, non-criminal friendships:

____

____

____

____

____

10. Understanding what victim harm is and how to make amends:

11. Taking personal responsibility for my actions:

12. Anything else I've learned from my treatment program:

Exercise 9.2: What I Have Learned About My Life Experiences, My Life Goals, My Offense Chain(s), and My Self-Regulation

Life Experiences and Predisposing Factors

Think about the personal history exercise you did in chapter 5. In that exercise and also in your treatment program, you will have learned about how your life experiences have shaped your life goals, any goals you have given up on, the problems you have experienced in life, and your offending behavior. Remember to include everything, whether it is from this workbook or from your treatment program.

1. As you have explored your personal history in treatment, what are some of the important things you have learned about how your life experiences have shaped your life goals that you haven't discussed elsewhere in this workbook?

____

____

____

____

____

2. How are you making changes to your life as a result of what you've learned overall?

____

____

____

____

____

Offense Chain

In this section, think about the offense chain or chains you developed in chapter 6. By this stage in treatment, you will have learned about your own pathways to offending and your self-regulation as well as how your pathways and self-regulation have influenced meeting your important life goals and your offending. You have probably learned additional helpful information from your therapist about yourself and during treatment, so you should include that information, as well.

1. As you have worked in treatment, what are some important things you have learned about your offense chain that you haven't covered in this workbook?

____

____

____

____

____

2. How are you making changes to your life as a result of what you've learned so far?

____

____

____

____

____

____

Self-Regulation

In chapter 3, you learned about your own self-regulation style. By this stage in treatment, you will have learned about how you respond and react to various situations and events in your life. You also will have learned how your self-regulation has influenced the ways you approach both your important life goals and your offending.

1. What have you learned about your self-regulation style in treatment that you haven't discussed in this workbook?

____

____

____

____

____

____

2. What changes are you making to your life as a result of what you've learned so far?

____

____

____

____

____

____

Exercise 9.3:
What I Have Learned About My Offense Pathways

Offense Pathways

In this section, you will be asked to use what you learned in chapters 6 and 7 about the offense pathway or pathways you followed in your offending. By this stage in treatment, you understand your offense pathway(s) very well, and have learned skills and strategies to increase your awareness and to monitor your thoughts, feelings, and emotions.

For each offense pathway, you can do specific things to manage your risk to re-offend and to meet your life goals. The next sections of the workbook will focus on what you have learned in treatment, enabling you to better develop specific strategies for each pathway. Even if you did not follow a certain pathway in your offending, review all of the information below, as some of the information may still be relevant to you. Also, during treatment, you will have developed skills and increased your understanding of your offending, and so information you provide about each pathway may be helpful.

Avoidant-Passive Offense Pathway

Remember from chapter 7 that a person follows the avoidant-passive pathway when he doesn't want to offend (an avoidance goal) but he doesn't use any strategies in the offense chain to prevent himself from offending (passive style). During the offense chain, the person feels more and more out of control, but does not really do anything about it. He is not able to cope with the events that happen during the offense chain. When he gets closer to offending, he gives up on his goal to avoid offending, and he approaches offending.

Wanting to avoid offending is very important; it is a good first step. But not being able to meet this goal puts you at very high risk for re-offending. At times, your motivation is likely to waiver. Your confidence about changing can dissolve, your ambivalence can come back, and you can find yourself placing less importance on making changes. One of the essential elements of change is keeping your motivation high for your avoidance goal, at all times, as well as getting your motivation back if it decreases or stops. Another essential element of change is using your skills and your self-regulation to keep in control when something happens that could trigger an offense chain.

What follow is a series of questions for you to think about. After the set of questions are two questions for you to answer about what you have learned so far. You will be reflecting on what you have learned in your treatment program as well as in this workbook.

1. What specific strategies have you developed to stay motivated to keep your avoidance goal?
2. What specific strategies have you developed to stay motivated to keep your avoidance goal in situations that are risky for re-offending?
3. What specific strategies have you developed to increase your motivation to keep your avoidance goal, if your motivation starts to decrease?
4. What would be the impact on your important life goals if you re-offended?
5. How can you use your motivation to have a good life and to keep your goal to avoid offending?
6. How can meeting your important life goals help you to reduce your risk to re-offend?
7. What life goals could you possibly lose if you were to re-offend?
8. What self-regulation strategies have you learned that will help you to keep your goal to avoid offending?
9. What are the benefits of keeping your goal to avoid offending?
10. What are the consequences to your good life plan of not keeping your goal to avoid offending?
11. How has your awareness of your offense chain changed in treatment? That is, what do you know now that you did not know before about why you offended and about how you responded during the offense chain?
12. How can you use this increased awareness of your offense chain to manage your risk and to prevent re-offending?
13. What specific strategies and skills have you learned in treatment to cope with losing control in risky situations for offending?
14. What specific strategies and skills have you learned in treatment that will help you to meet your important life goals without re-offending?
15. What have you learned about how your schemas, attitudes, and beliefs relate to your offense chain? How can you use what you have learned to prevent re-offending?
16. What problem-solving skills have you learned and how will you apply these skills to prevent re-offending?
17. What self-regulation skills for impulsivity, emotions, sexual arousal, and other risk factors have you learned? How will you apply these skills to help you prevent re-offending?
18. What strategies do you have in place to help you escape from high-risk situations?

19. How can you use self-monitoring of your thoughts, emotions, and behavior to help you prevent offending?
20. How will you know when you are thinking in problematic ways? What can you do and what will you do about those ways of thinking? Be specific.
21. What skills and strategies have you developed in order to cope with stress and with problems that come up in your life?
22. What important life goals were you meeting by offending and how will you meet those goals without offending?

As you think about the previous questions and your answers to them, please answer the questions that follow:

1. What have you learned about the avoidant-passive pathway in treatment that you haven't discussed yet in this workbook?

____

____

____

____

____

____

____

____

____

____

____

____

____

2. How are you making changes to your life as a result of what you've learned about this pathway?

____

____

____

____

____

____

____

____

____

____

Avoidant-Active Pathway

Remember from chapter 7 that a person following the avoidant-active pathway does not want to offend (avoidance goal), and he tries to do something in order not to offend (active style). His strategies are not effective, however, and they sometimes increase his risk. Maybe he tried to cope with his emotions by using drugs or alcohol, but doing this actually resulted in a loss of control. Or maybe he tried to use pornography instead of acting out on someone, but the pornography just made him think about sex even more. During the offense chain, he feels more and more of a loss of control when his strategies to cope don't work. When he gets closer to offending, he gives up on his goal to avoid offending, and he approaches or moves toward offending, instead.

What follow is a series of questions for you to think about. After the set of questions are two questions for you to answer about what you have learned so far, in your treatment pro gram as well as in this workbook.

1. What specific strategies have you developed to stay motivated to keep your avoidance goal?
2. What specific strategies have you developed to stay motivated to keep your avoidance goal in situations that are risky for re-offending?
3. How has your awareness of your ineffective strategies increased during treatment?
4. What new strategies have you learned in order to prevent offending successfully?
5. What have you learned in treatment that will make sure you are able to keep your avoidance goal when you find yourself in risky situations?
6. What have you learned in treatment that will make sure you do not give up if your strategies do not work?
7. What new strategies have you learned that will help you prevent re-offending?

8. How can these strategies help you to meet your important life goals without offending?
9. How can you apply these strategies to solving other problems that come up in your life?
10. How can you apply these strategies to make sure that you meet your important goals in life in positive ways and without offending?
11. How can you apply these strategies to change your self-regulation style so that you become more controlled in your style?
12. What important life goals were you meeting by offending, and how will you meet these goals without offending?
13. How will you use self-monitoring to make sure that the new skills to prevent offending that you have mastered are working and are helping you to manage your thoughts, feelings, and behavior?
14. What have you learned about using ineffective skills in other areas of your life? That is, what have you learned in treatment about how common it is for you, in general, to use strategies that don't work to solve your problems and to meet your goals?
15. What new, better skills have you developed during treatment, and how will you use these in your life in general?
16. How will you use those skills to manage your risk factors and prevent re-offending?

As you think about the previous questions and your answers to them, please answer the following questions:

1. What have you learned about the avoidant-active pathway in treatment that you haven't discussed yet in this workbook?

____

____

____

____

____

____

____

____

2. How are you making changes to your life as a result of what you've learned about this pathway?

____

____

____

____

____

____

____

____

____

Approach-Automatic Pathway

Remember from chapter 7 that the person following this pathway believes offending is okay and he doesn't want to prevent offending from happening in a situation (approach goal). When a high-risk situation happens, he reacts to what is happening around him at the time (automatic style). Sometimes he reacts impulsively, without a lot of planning. Other times, he sees an opportunity and acts on it by offending. This person meets his goals by offending.

What follows is a series of questions for you to think about. After the set of questions are two questions for you to answer about what you have learned so far in your treatment program as well as in this workbook.

1. What have you learned about how your problematic schemas, attitudes, and beliefs developed in your life? That is, why did you initially develop these attitudes and beliefs? What purpose did they serve?
2. How do these schemas, attitudes, and beliefs lead you to offending?
3. How do these schemas, attitudes, and beliefs lead to your life problems?
4. What have you learned about the pros and cons of these attitudes, beliefs, and schemas? That is, how do they work to help you meet your goals and how do they interfere with meeting your goals?
5. What strategies have you learned to manage how you respond and react when you start to use problematic schemas or attitudes?

6. How will you use self-monitoring to manage your schemas and attitudes?
7. What have you learned in treatment about changing your schemas and attitudes in order to avoid life problems and to prevent offending?
8. How have you managed to change your offense approach goal to an avoidance goal?
9. What strategies have you learned to ensure you will keep an avoidance goal and not go back to your approach goal?
10. What specific skills and strategies have you learned to help you manage impulsivity?
11. What skills and strategies have you learned in order to deal with cues in the situation or the environment that might trigger your problematic attitudes and schemas?
12. What work do you still need to do in treatment and when you are under supervision to continue to change and manage your schemas and attitudes?
13. How can others help you to stay on track?
14. How will you know when situations or other people activate your schemas?
15. How will you manage your schemas when they are being activated?
16. How will you know when your schemas and attitudes are interfering with meeting your important life goals?
17. What skills have you learned to be able to manage this interference so that you don't offend and so that you meet your goals?
18. What important life goals were you meeting by offending?
19. How will you meet these goals without offending?
20. How can you use your new avoidance goal to meet your important life goals without offending?

As you think about the previous questions and your answers to them, please answer the following questions:

1. What have you learned about the approach-automatic pathway in treatment that you haven't discussed yet in this workbook?

____

____

____

____

____

____

____

____

____

2. How are you making changes to your life as a result of what you've learned about this pathway?

____

____

____

____

____

____

____

____

____

Approach-Explicit Pathway

Remember from chapter 7 that the person following this pathway has the attitude that offending is okay (approach goal), and he plans his offenses in order to meet his needs and goals (explicit style). To him, acting out is a positive experience.

Below is a series of questions for you to think about. After the set of questions are two questions for you to answer about what you have learned so far, both in your treatment program as well as in this workbook.

1. What have you learned about your sexual interests and urges?
2. How can you use your controlled self-regulation to help you to lead an abuse-free lifestyle?
3. What have you learned about how your problematic schemas, attitudes, and beliefs developed in your life? That is, why did you initially develop these attitudes and beliefs? What purpose did they serve?
4. How do these schemas, attitudes, and beliefs lead to offending?
5. How do these schemas, attitudes, and beliefs lead to your life problems?
6. What have you learned about the pros and cons of these attitudes, beliefs, and schemas? That is, how do they work to help you meet your goals and how do they interfere with meeting your goals?
7. What strategies have you learned for managing how you respond and react when you start to use problematic schemas or attitudes?
8. How will you use self-monitoring to manage your schemas and attitudes?
9. What have you learned in treatment about changing your schemas and attitudes in order to avoid life problems and to prevent offending?
10. How have you managed to change your offense approach goal to an avoidance goal?
11. What strategies have you learned to ensure that you will keep your new avoidance goal and not go back to your approach goal?
12. What skills and strategies have you learned in order to deal with cues in the situation or environment that trigger your problematic attitudes and schemas?
13. What work do you still need to do in treatment and supervision to continue to change and manage your schemas and attitudes?
14. How can others help you to stay on track?
15. How will you know when situations and other people activate your schemas? How will you manage these situations?
16. How will you know when your schemas and attitudes are interfering with meeting your important life goals? What skills have you learned to be able to manage this interference so that you don't offend and so that you meet your goals?

17. What important life goals were you meeting by offending and how will you meet these goals without offending?

18. How can you use your new avoidance goal and your controlled self-regulation to meet your important life goals without offending?

As you think about the previous questions and your answers to them, answer the following questions:

1. What have you learned about the approach-explicit pathway in treatment that you haven't discussed yet in this workbook?

2. How are you making changes to your life as a result of what you've learned about this pathway?

Summary

In this section, you have looked at specific things you have learned and skills you have developed in your treatment program. Some of these topics are not addressed in this workbook, but they are related to your progress. You have pulled together material that you have learned both in treatment and in this workbook. This material will be important to your work in the next chapters of this workbook, which will focus on developing your risk management plan and your good life plan, and implementing your plans in the community.

CHAPTER 10

My Risk Management Plan

So far in this workbook and in treatment, you have examined a great deal of information in detail about yourself and your life. You've learned about your goals, your self-regulation style, your personal history, offense patterns and pathways, and your motivation to make important changes in your life. In this part of the book, you will put this knowledge together and learn specific actions you can put into your risk management plan. In chapter 11, you will work on developing your good life plan. Both your risk management plan and your good life plan are essential to your success in changing because this is how you will live your life in a healthy, satisfying way and effectively manage your risk to re-offend.

In working on the exercises in this chapter, you should include everything you have learned so far in treatment and in this workbook. By this stage, you will have a very good understanding of who you are, who you want to be, and what challenges or obstacles you face. You should also be well on your way toward having new strategies to meet your life goals and to deal with your problems.

Keep in mind that not everything in your risk management plan is from this workbook. You will need to work with your therapist and case management team to include everything that is important in your plan.

Motivation

In chapter 1, you looked at your motivation to embark on personal change. In chapter 8, you looked at how your motivation has changed over time and during treatment. What you choose to do during those times when your motivation is lower—for whatever reason—is very important. Motivation means your motivation to meet your goals, to prevent and cope with your life problems, and to manage your risk. It is very important to plan for challenging times, because you can expect for certain these challenges will happen—they happen to everyone. Ideally, your motivation to change your life is high most of the time, because you have decided that having a better life and not offending is important to you, and because you have learned and practiced the skills you need to achieve this goal. But, even when you've reached that decision, certain situations or events may lower your motivation. So part of your change plan is learning how to be prepared to cope with those times when they happen.

Exercise 10.1: Maintaining My Motivation

Recall from chapter 1 that three key elements are related to motivation: *the importance of change*, *your confidence in your ability to change*, and *your ambivalence about making change*. The following exercise addresses all three of these topics. As you answer the following questions, be honest with yourself and also be specific about what you will do in these areas.

Importance of Change

Using the following chart, first describe all of the specific situations unique to you that could lower your motivation to change. Also list situations when keeping your motivation or following your plans might not seem as important. Then, write your strategies to manage each situation, describing what you will do in order to increase your motivation again in each of those situations. It is important to be specific.

SITUATION	WHAT I WILL DO TO KEEP CHANGE IMPORTANT TO ME AND INCREASE MY MOTIVATION
#1 ______________________	1. ______________________
______________________	______________________
______________________	2. ______________________
______________________	______________________
______________________	3. ______________________
______________________	______________________
______________________	4. ______________________
______________________	______________________
______________________	5. ______________________
______________________	______________________
#2 ______________________	1. ______________________
______________________	______________________
______________________	2. ______________________
______________________	______________________
______________________	3. ______________________
______________________	______________________
______________________	4. ______________________
______________________	______________________
______________________	5. ______________________
______________________	______________________

Continued on next page

SITUATION	WHAT I WILL DO TO KEEP CHANGE IMPORTANT TO ME AND INCREASE MY MOTIVATION
#3 ______	1. ______ 2. ______ 3. ______ 4. ______ 5. ______
#4 ______	1. ______ 2. ______ 3. ______ 4. ______ 5. ______

SITUATION	WHAT I WILL DO TO KEEP CHANGE IMPORTANT TO ME AND INCREASE MY MOTIVATION
#5 ______	1. ______
	2. ______
	3. ______
	4. ______
	5. ______
#6 ______	1. ______
	2. ______
	3. ______
	4. ______
	5. ______

Continued on next page

SITUATION	WHAT I WILL DO TO KEEP CHANGE IMPORTANT TO ME AND INCREASE MY MOTIVATION
#7 ______	1. ______ ______ 2. ______ ______ 3. ______ ______ 4. ______ ______ 5. ______ ______
#8 ______	1. ______ ______ 2. ______ ______ 3. ______ ______ 4. ______ ______ 5. ______ ______

SITUATION	WHAT I WILL DO TO KEEP CHANGE IMPORTANT TO ME AND INCREASE MY MOTIVATION
#9 ______ ______ ______ ______ ______ ______ ______ ______ ______ ______	1. ______ ______ 2. ______ ______ 3. ______ ______ 4. ______ ______ 5. ______ ______
#10 ______ ______ ______ ______ ______ ______ ______ ______ ______ ______	1. ______ ______ 2. ______ ______ 3. ______ ______ 4. ______ ______ 5. ______ ______

Confidence in Being Able to Change

Now, think about your confidence about being able to actually change. Using the chart that follows, first write all of the specific situations in which your confidence about being able to change might decrease from what it is now or from your ideal level. What you write can be based on your past experiences as well as on new situations you have learned about that could affect you. Next, write your strategies to manage each situation, describing what you will do in order to increase your confidence again in that situation. Again, please be specific.

SITUATION	WHAT I WILL DO TO KEEP MY CONFIDENCE ABOUT BEING ABLE TO CHANGE
#1 ______________________	1. ______________________
______________________	______________________
______________________	2. ______________________
______________________	______________________
______________________	3. ______________________
______________________	______________________
______________________	4. ______________________
______________________	______________________
______________________	5. ______________________
______________________	______________________

SITUATION	WHAT I WILL DO TO KEEP MY CONFIDENCE ABOUT BEING ABLE TO CHANGE
#2 ______________ ______________ ______________ ______________ ______________ ______________ ______________ ______________ ______________ ______________	1. ______________ ______________ 2. ______________ ______________ 3. ______________ ______________ 4. ______________ ______________ 5. ______________ ______________
#3 ______________ ______________ ______________ ______________ ______________ ______________ ______________ ______________ ______________ ______________	1. ______________ ______________ 2. ______________ ______________ 3. ______________ ______________ 4. ______________ ______________ 5. ______________ ______________

Continued on next page

SITUATION	WHAT I WILL DO TO KEEP MY CONFIDENCE ABOUT BEING ABLE TO CHANGE
#4 ______________________	1. ______________________ ______________________ 2. ______________________ ______________________ 3. ______________________ ______________________ 4. ______________________ ______________________ 5. ______________________ ______________________
#5 ______________________	1. ______________________ ______________________ 2. ______________________ ______________________ 3. ______________________ ______________________ 4. ______________________ ______________________ 5. ______________________ ______________________

SITUATION	WHAT I WILL DO TO KEEP MY CONFIDENCE ABOUT BEING ABLE TO CHANGE
#6 ______________	1. ______________ ______________ 2. ______________ ______________ 3. ______________ ______________ 4. ______________ ______________ 5. ______________ ______________
#7 ______________	1. ______________ ______________ 2. ______________ ______________ 3. ______________ ______________ 4. ______________ ______________ 5. ______________ ______________

Continued on next page

SITUATION	WHAT I WILL DO TO KEEP MY CONFIDENCE ABOUT BEING ABLE TO CHANGE
#8 ______	1. ______ 2. ______ 3. ______ 4. ______ 5. ______
#9 ______	1. ______ 2. ______ 3. ______ 4. ______ 5. ______

SITUATION	WHAT I WILL DO TO KEEP MY CONFIDENCE ABOUT BEING ABLE TO CHANGE
#10 __________	1. __________
__________	__________
__________	2. __________
__________	__________
__________	3. __________
__________	__________
__________	4. __________
__________	__________
__________	5. __________
__________	__________

Ambivalence About Change

Lastly, think about times when you might be ambivalent about change, those times when you feel pulled in different directions about whether or not change is worth pursuing. Using the chart that follows, first describe all of the specific situations in which you become or might become ambivalent about making changes. Then, write your strategies to manage each situation, describing what you will do in order to tip the balance back in favor of changing in that situation. Again, it is important to be specific.

SITUATION	WHAT I WILL DO TO COPE WITH MY AMBIVALENCE ABOUT CHANGE
#1 ______	1. ______
	2. ______
	3. ______
	4. ______
	5. ______
#2 ______	1. ______
	2. ______
	3. ______
	4. ______
	5. ______

SITUATION	WHAT I WILL DO TO COPE WITH MY AMBIVALENCE ABOUT CHANGE
#3 ____________	1. ____________ ____________ 2. ____________ ____________ 3. ____________ ____________ 4. ____________ ____________ 5. ____________ ____________
#4 ____________	1. ____________ ____________ 2. ____________ ____________ 3. ____________ ____________ 4. ____________ ____________ 5. ____________ ____________

Continued on next page

SITUATION	WHAT I WILL DO TO COPE WITH MY AMBIVALENCE ABOUT CHANGE
#5 ____________	1. ____________ ____________ 2. ____________ ____________ 3. ____________ ____________ 4. ____________ ____________ 5. ____________ ____________
#6 ____________	1. ____________ ____________ 2. ____________ ____________ 3. ____________ ____________ 4. ____________ ____________ 5. ____________ ____________

SITUATION	WHAT I WILL DO TO COPE WITH MY AMBIVALENCE ABOUT CHANGE
#7	1. 2. 3. 4. 5.
#8	1. 2. 3. 4. 5.

Continued on next page

SITUATION	WHAT I WILL DO TO COPE WITH MY AMBIVALENCE ABOUT CHANGE
#9	1. 2. 3. 4. 5.
#10	1. 2. 3. 4. 5.

Change Language

Recall from chapter 1 that part of implementing change is your change language—what you tell yourself and others that both reflects and reinforces your commitment to change. Change language (sometimes called "change talk") typically comes in statements about *desire*, *ability*, *reason*, and *need* to change. Recall that this change language will help you maintain your motivation and help you when your motivation to change decreases. In this section, write your most effective change language statements. By this stage in treatment, it is anticipated that you are using these on a regular basis—every day.

My Change Language Statements:

1. ______________________________
2. ______________________________
3. ______________________________
4. ______________________________
5. ______________________________
6. ______________________________
7. ______________________________
8. ______________________________
9. ______________________________
10. ______________________________

Risk Factors

While your self-regulation plan should include your good life plan and ways to ensure that you don't meet your goals through offending, part of your self-regulation plan is also to manage your risk factors. These factors are especially important for your success. You explored your own risk factors in depth in chapter 4. This next exercise is different from what you did in those exercises because it deals specifically with your strategies for managing your risk factors. In this exercise, you will indicate your risk factors, the strategies you have developed to manage your risk factors, and the strategies you are still working on developing or improving. Do not think about your goals or your good life plan here. Focus only on your risk factors from chapter 4 and what you have learned in treatment.

MY RISK FACTOR #1	
MY STRATEGIES	
STRATEGIES I NEED TO DEVELOP OR IMPROVE	

MY RISK FACTOR #2	
MY STRATEGIES	
STRATEGIES I NEED TO DEVELOP OR IMPROVE	

MY RISK FACTOR #3	______ ______ ______
MY STRATEGIES	______ ______ ______
STRATEGIES I NEED TO DEVELOP OR IMPROVE	______ ______ ______

MY RISK FACTOR #4	______ ______ ______
MY STRATEGIES	______ ______ ______
STRATEGIES I NEED TO DEVELOP OR IMPROVE	______ ______ ______

Continued on next page

MY RISK FACTOR #5	
MY STRATEGIES	
STRATEGIES I NEED TO DEVELOP OR IMPROVE	

MY RISK FACTOR #6	
MY STRATEGIES	
STRATEGIES I NEED TO DEVELOP OR IMPROVE	

MY RISK FACTOR #7	
MY STRATEGIES	
STRATEGIES I NEED TO DEVELOP OR IMPROVE	

MY RISK FACTOR #8	
MY STRATEGIES	
STRATEGIES I NEED TO DEVELOP OR IMPROVE	

Continued on next page

MY RISK FACTOR #9	
MY STRATEGIES	
STRATEGIES I NEED TO DEVELOP OR IMPROVE	

MY RISK FACTOR #10	
MY STRATEGIES	
STRATEGIES I NEED TO DEVELOP OR IMPROVE	

Exercise 10.2: My Goals in Offending

In analyzing your offense pathway and your offense chain, you also learned about the common life goals you were trying to gain through offending. Part of managing your risk is learning how to meet these goals in ways that don't involve offending. In exercise 6.7, you explored each of the steps in your offense chain. In this exercise, you will focus on your goals in each step of the chain. What did you want to happen? What did you want to accomplish or to achieve? Using the diagram that follows, write your goals at each stage of the offense chain.

Step 1: My Goals When the Life Event Happened
1. ______
2. ______
3. ______

↓

Step 2: My Goals When I Reacted to the Life Event
1. ______
2. ______
3. ______

↓

Step 3: Goals That I Wanted in the Situation
1. ______
2. ______
3. ______

↓

Step 4: My Goals When I Used My Strategies
1. ______
2. ______
3. ______

↓

Continued on next page

Step 5: My Goals in the High-Risk Situation

1. ______________________________

2. ______________________________

3. ______________________________

↓

Step 6: My Goals Right Before Offending

1. ______________________________

2. ______________________________

3. ______________________________

↓

Step 7: My Goals During Offending

1. ______________________________

2. ______________________________

3. ______________________________

↓

Step 8: My Short-Term Goals Right After Offending

1. ______________________________

2. ______________________________

3. ______________________________

↓

Step 9: My Long-Term Goals After Offending

1. ______________________________

2. ______________________________

3. ______________________________

Next, in the chart that follows, write all the goals from the offense chain that you just finished doing above. Then, write the strategies you have developed so you do not meet your goals by offending. Last, write the strategies that you need to develop further or improve. Be sure to include strategies that you plan to use to meet your life goals in ways other than offending.

MY GOALS DURING THE OFFENSE CHAIN #1	
MY STRATEGIES TO NOT MEET MY GOALS BY OFFENDING	
STRATEGIES I NEED TO DEVELOP OR IMPROVE	

MY GOALS DURING THE OFFENSE CHAIN #2	
MY STRATEGIES TO NOT MEET MY GOALS BY OFFENDING	
STRATEGIES I NEED TO DEVELOP OR IMPROVE	

Continued on next page

MY GOALS DURING THE OFFENSE CHAIN #3	______ ______ ______
MY STRATEGIES TO NOT MEET MY GOALS BY OFFENDING	______ ______ ______
STRATEGIES I NEED TO DEVELOP OR IMPROVE	______ ______ ______

MY GOALS DURING THE OFFENSE CHAIN #4	______ ______ ______
MY STRATEGIES TO NOT MEET MY GOALS BY OFFENDING	______ ______ ______
STRATEGIES I NEED TO DEVELOP OR IMPROVE	______ ______ ______

MY GOALS DURING THE OFFENSE CHAIN #5	________________ ________________ ________________
MY STRATEGIES TO NOT MEET MY GOALS BY OFFENDING	________________ ________________ ________________
STRATEGIES I NEED TO DEVELOP OR IMPROVE	________________ ________________ ________________

MY GOALS DURING THE OFFENSE CHAIN #6	________________ ________________ ________________
MY STRATEGIES TO NOT MEET MY GOALS BY OFFENDING	________________ ________________ ________________
STRATEGIES I NEED TO DEVELOP OR IMPROVE	________________ ________________ ________________

Continued on next page

MY GOALS DURING THE OFFENSE CHAIN #7	
MY STRATEGIES TO NOT MEET MY GOALS BY OFFENDING	
STRATEGIES I NEED TO DEVELOP OR IMPROVE	

MY GOALS DURING THE OFFENSE CHAIN #8	
MY STRATEGIES TO NOT MEET MY GOALS BY OFFENDING	
STRATEGIES I NEED TO DEVELOP OR IMPROVE	

MY GOALS DURING THE OFFENSE CHAIN #9	
MY STRATEGIES TO NOT MEET MY GOALS BY OFFENDING	
STRATEGIES I NEED TO DEVELOP OR IMPROVE	

MY GOALS DURING THE OFFENSE CHAIN #10	
MY STRATEGIES TO NOT MEET MY GOALS BY OFFENDING	
STRATEGIES I NEED TO DEVELOP OR IMPROVE	

Continued on next page

Self-Regulation

In chapter 3, you looked at your self-regulation style and patterns of responding. Your self-regulation style applied to your life and also to your offending. In chapter 8, you looked at your progress in this area, how you have changed, and what is left for you to do. In the section below, you will be pulling all of this material together into a specific self-management plan that will be part of your risk management plan.

Exercise 10.3: My Self-Regulation Plan

Below are some statements about self-regulation style. For this first part of the exercise, check how each statement applies to you—whether it applies rarely, sometimes, or often. It is important for you to think about your patterns overall in your life and not just at this point in treatment, when you are better able to manage yourself. The reason for looking at the whole picture is because your responses are well-established patterns, and they could emerge again in the future and put you at high risk to re-offend.

1. I am able to monitor my behavior:
   ☐ Rarely ☐ Sometimes ☐ Often

2. I am able to monitor what I am thinking:
   ☐ Rarely ☐ Sometimes ☐ Often

3. I am able to monitor what I am feeling (my emotions):
   ☐ Rarely ☐ Sometimes ☐ Often

4. I am able to cope with problems that happen in my life:
   ☐ Rarely ☐ Sometimes ☐ Often

5. I am able to cope with my emotions:
   ☐ Rarely ☐ Sometimes ☐ Often

6. I am able to solve problems:
   ☐ Rarely ☐ Sometimes ☐ Often

7. I am able to weigh the pros and cons of what I should do in different situations:
   ☐ Rarely ☐ Sometimes ☐ Often

8. I am able to plan what I do:
   ☐ Rarely ☐ Sometimes ☐ Often

9. I am able to manage my impulsivity:
   ☐ Rarely ☐ Sometimes ☐ Often

10. I am able to set plans to achieve my goals:
   ☐ Rarely ☐ Sometimes ☐ Often

11. I am aware of what I am doing or thinking:
   ☐ Rarely ☐ Sometimes ☐ Often

12. I feel in control when I have problems:
   ☐ Rarely ☐ Sometimes ☐ Often

13. I use my skills to manage my behavior:
   ☐ Rarely ☐ Sometimes ☐ Often

14. I use my skills to manage my thinking:
   ☐ Rarely ☐ Sometimes ☐ Often

15. I use my skills to manage my emotions:
   ☐ Rarely ☐ Sometimes ☐ Often

16. I use my skills to solve problems:
   ☐ Rarely ☐ Sometimes ☐ Often

17. Situations that happen to me trigger problematic schemas, attitudes, and beliefs, but I am able to manage them:
   ☐ Rarely ☐ Sometimes ☐ Often

18. I am able to develop social relationships with people:
   ☐ Rarely ☐ Sometimes ☐ Often

19. I am able to develop intimate relationships:
   ☐ Rarely ☐ Sometimes ☐ Often

20. I sometimes feel overconfident in some situations:
   ☐ Rarely ☐ Sometimes ☐ Often

21. Now, look back at your answers and write the specific strategies you have learned so far to manage yourself in each area. Then write additional strategies you are working on now or that you need to improve in order to achieve effective self-regulation.

SKILL Coping with what happens to me in life	
My Strategies	Strategies I Need to Develop or Improve
1. ______	1. ______
2. ______	2. ______
3. ______	3. ______
4. ______	4. ______
5. ______	5. ______

SKILL Coping with my emotions	
My Strategies	Strategies I Need to Develop or Improve
1. ______	1. ______
2. ______	2. ______
3. ______	3. ______
4. ______	4. ______
5. ______	5. ______

SKILL Developing social relationships with people

My Strategies	Strategies I Need to Develop or Improve
1. ________	1. ________
2. ________	2. ________
3. ________	3. ________
4. ________	4. ________
5. ________	5. ________

SKILL Developing intimate relationships

My Strategies	Strategies I Need to Develop or Improve
1. ________	1. ________
2. ________	2. ________
3. ________	3. ________
4. ________	4. ________
5. ________	5. ________

Continued on next page

SKILL Monitoring my behavior

My Strategies	Strategies I Need to Develop or Improve
1. ____________	1. ____________
2. ____________	2. ____________
3. ____________	3. ____________
4. ____________	4. ____________
5. ____________	5. ____________

SKILL Monitoring what I am thinking

My Strategies	Strategies I Need to Develop or Improve
1. ____________	1. ____________
2. ____________	2. ____________
3. ____________	3. ____________
4. ____________	4. ____________
5. ____________	5. ____________

SKILL Monitoring what I am feeling	
My Strategies	Strategies I Need to Develop or Improve
1. ______________________	1. ______________________
______________________	______________________
2. ______________________	2. ______________________
______________________	______________________
3. ______________________	3. ______________________
______________________	______________________
4. ______________________	4. ______________________
______________________	______________________
5. ______________________	5. ______________________
______________________	______________________

For the last part of this exercise, go back over the list and put a check mark by all of the statements that could pose a risk for you for re-offending.

Offense Chain and Offense Pathways

As you have learned, a person's pathway to offending is related to his self-regulation style. Recall that the four pathways are a combination of goals and self-regulation strategies in an offending situation. In chapter 7, you learned about your own pathway or pathways when you offended. In chapter 4, you learned about your risk factors, and in chapter 9, you developed strategies to manage your risk. By this time in treatment, you will have a very good idea as to what your strengths are, what your problem areas are, what could lead you back to offending, and what you will do to reduce and manage your risk. In this section, you will combine all of this information together to develop your *risk management plan* to prevent offending again. This plan is meant to be implemented with your good life plan, which you will develop in chapter 11.

Exercise 10.4: My Offense Chain

1. Put a check mark or check marks beside your pathway(s) that you determined in chapter 7:

   ☐ Avoidant-Passive ☐ Approach-Automatic

   ☐ Avoidant-Active ☐ Approach-Explicit

2. When you analyzed your pathway and your offense chain in chapters 6 and 7, what were the important things you learned about your offending patterns and how they are related to your pathway or pathways?

____

____

____

____

____

____

____

____

____

____

____

____

____

____

____

____

____

____

Exercise 10.5: My Risk Management Plan

Now, it is time to bring everything together into your own personal plan to manage your risk to re-offend. By this point, you should know all of your risks and goals in offending and know what you need to do to avoid re-offending. You will have developed good strategies and will be aware of other strategies you still need to work on or improve. In this section you will put together many of the elements you have explored separately throughout this workbook. These elements include the risk factors that are relevant to you, the goals you have when these factors are present, the related common life goals that are linked to your risk factors (which you explored in exercise 4.2), the self-regulation skills you can use, and the specific strategies you can use. Please include any other topics you have learned about in treatment that are important, including such things as taking responsibility, substance abuse, mental health, and so forth.

To assist you in this exercise, let's return to the case of Jay, in chapter 7. Remember that when he entered treatment, Jay had few emotional connections to others, and he viewed the world as a place where one has to have fun when opportunities arise. He also saw the world as a place in which authorities can be hostile, controlling, and unpredictable. Jay forced sex onto younger teens when the staff of his juvenile program wasn't looking. He saw opportunities when they presented themselves and his attitude toward his assaults was that the behavior itself was fun and worth the risk.

Jay later sexually assaulted a woman in the bathroom of a bar. He believed that women could not be trusted to tell the truth, particularly in sexual matters. He believed that this woman had flirted with him, so it made little difference to him that he assaulted her. His view was, "She owed me." He had actually not had any particular plans in advance to assault anyone that evening. Jay felt positive about his actions of that evening because he had met his goals. To others, this assault seemed to come from "out of the blue."

A beginning account for Jay of his risk factors, goals, skills, and strategies might look like the first chart that follows. The chart is not complete, but it is provided to give you some guidance in completing your own chart.

You will find a chart like Jay's for you to fill out beginning on page 352. Start by listing your risk factors, and then write out the goals you have (for when this factor is operating) and your related common life goals. The purpose is to help you make the links between your life goals and your risk factors. Next, write out the self-regulation skills and specific strategies you have learned and that you can use to manage the risk factors. You should seek out the help of your therapist to make sure you are completing this fully.

RISK FACTOR	Abuse-related schemas, including that women deserve to be raped

GOALS I HAVE WHEN THIS FACTOR IS HAPPENING	RELATED COMMON LIFE GOALS
To have sex	Peace of mind, happiness
To get what I think is coming to me	Personal choice and independence
To see myself as a tough guy	Personal choice and independence happiness, peace of mind

SKILLS AND SELF-REGULATION STRATEGIES I WILL USE

I will use self-monitoring strategies so I know when I am thinking this way.

I will use my problem-solving/thinking skills, particularly stopping and thinking.

I will use my arousal control techniques and skills.

I can take a time-out to regain control.

I will review motivation exercises in this workbook and use my change talk.

I will implement my strategies that are options for other ways I can feel independent, happy, and have peace of mind.

I will return to my good life plan to review conflicts/problems with goals and implement my action plan.

Talk to my PO and support persons.

I will remind myself that this is an "old me" thinking style.

I will remind myself of who I am now and how different I am from who I was then.

I will remind myself that this is a conflict between my goals of independence, happiness, and personal choice.

I will remind myself that offending gets in the way of my long-term goals.

I will focus on building relationships instead of just sex.

I will remind myself of the consequences of offending.

I will remind myself and be aware of what I am thinking and doing at all times.

I will remind myself that I can have happiness, independence, and peace of mind without sex and without hurting others.

I will continually monitor and challenge my abuse-related schemas and cognitive distortions.

I will seek out others for help and seek validation for keeping myself out of trouble.

I will take a few minutes every day to reflect on my accomplishments.

I will celebrate the fact that I now recognize possibilities for trouble and manage them without acting out.

RISK FACTOR	
GOALS I HAVE WHEN THIS FACTOR IS HAPPENING	RELATED COMMON LIFE GOALS

SKILLS AND SELF-REGULATION STRATEGIES I WILL USE

RISK FACTOR	
GOALS I HAVE WHEN THIS FACTOR IS HAPPENING	RELATED COMMON LIFE GOALS
SKILLS AND SELF-REGULATION STRATEGIES I WILL USE	

RISK FACTOR	
GOALS I HAVE WHEN THIS FACTOR IS HAPPENING	RELATED COMMON LIFE GOALS

SKILLS AND SELF-REGULATION STRATEGIES I WILL USE

Summary

Congratulations! You have now constructed your risk management plan. This plan will be an important part of your success, as well as a guide for your work with others, whether they be therapists, community supervision agents, or support persons. In the next chapter of the workbook, you will finalize your good life plan. After that, you will finish everything off by working on how you will implement your plan in the community.

CHAPTER 11

My Good Life Plan

Now that you are nearing the end of this workbook, it is time to put together your good life plan. For this section, you will need to return to the exercises you completed in chapter 2 to review what you wrote then. In chapter 2 you focused on your good life plans in the past and started to look at your good life plan in the future. it may be possible that you have a new perspective on many of these same questions. The task in this chapter is not to repeat the same answers you gave before but to go back over these elements of your treatment to ensure that you are on the right track as you move forward to develop your good life plan from now into the future, and to include any changes. As with every other part of this workbook, it will also be vital to discuss these exercises with your therapist as you proceed.

Earlier in this workbook, you learned about important common life goals that form your good life plan or roadmap for living. This plan included things that were important to you in the past and things that are important to you now. Also, your plan included what you do to meet these goals and the situations in which meeting your goals does not work as planned or causes problems in your life or leads to offending. At this point in treatment, you have also learned about your risk factors for offending, your offense pathway(s), and the things you want and need to change in order to have a good life and to reduce your risk to re-offend. In this part of the workbook, you will bring together your goals and your strategies to meet these goals, including risk management strategies you have developed. It is important to note, however, that neither this plan nor the risk management plan you created in chapter 10 is the final word in either your attempts to live a better life or your plans to manage risk. The various elements of your plans are likely to change over time and with changes in your life. In the next part of this workbook, you will address how to implement your plan and how to troubleshoot when things do not go as planned. You will also address how to use your plans to manage your risk in the future.

Recall that your good life plan represents what is important to you in your life, where you would like to go from here, and how you will get to that place. It is made up of all of the 10 common life goals laid out in a balanced and complete way and so you can meet these goals in satisfying, healthy ways without offending.

At this stage, it will be important for you to review your important goals, flaws in your good life plan, and the new strategies you have developed to meet your life goals. You also worked on the strategies you used earlier in your life, including some strategies that worked well. You can include those strategies here, too.

As you work on the exercises to come, think about how important each of the common life goals you identified is to you and what plans you have developed in order to achieve these goals in a healthy way that will enhance your life and prevent life problems. When you work on these exercises, it is important to be specific.

The exercises that follow will focus on your good life plan *from now on*. The plan can include goals that were important to you in the past as well as goals that you previously gave up but have rediscovered. The plan will also include your strategies for implementing your good life plan, exploring how you and others will know that you are on track with your plan, and looking at things that could result in problems or in increased risk.

Exercise 11.1: My Good Life

As you have learned so far in treatment and by using this workbook, everyone has a different idea of what a good life is. Before looking at the specific elements of your good life plan, think about how you see yourself and your life in general.

1. What is your vision overall of what your good life will look like, based on what you have learned about the goals that are important in your life now?

____

____

____

____

____

____

____

____

Exercise 11.2: Meeting My Important Goals

In chapter 2 of this workbook, you identified your goals in the past as well as your goals now. This next exercise is about your goals *now and for the future* and it will form the basis of your good life plan. This plan is what you will implement from now on with strategies you have learned in treatment, along with your risk management plan from chapter 10.

To start, review the 10 common life goals from the chart in chapter 2 and then describe your goals for the future for each of the 10 goals. After that, indicate what priority the common goal has in your life now, with 1 being the highest priority and 10 being the lowest priority. Last, describe specifically what you will do to meet each goal. To be successful in meeting your goals, it is important that you be specific in your plans.

COMMON LIFE GOAL Life: Living and Surviving
PRIORITY (1 = HIGHEST, 10 = LOWEST) ☐
HOW I WILL MEET THIS GOAL (WHAT I WILL DO)
1. __________ 2. __________ 3. __________ 4. __________ 5. __________

Continued on next page

COMMON LIFE GOAL Knowledge: Learning and Knowing

PRIORITY (1 = HIGHEST, 10 = LOWEST) ☐

HOW I WILL MEET THIS GOAL
(WHAT I WILL DO)

1. ______________________________

2. ______________________________

3. ______________________________

4. ______________________________

5. ______________________________

COMMON LIFE GOAL Being Good at Work and Play

PRIORITY (1 = HIGHEST, 10 = LOWEST) ☐

HOW I WILL MEET THIS GOAL
(WHAT I WILL DO)

1. ______________________________

2. ______________________________

3. ______________________________

4. ______________________________

5. ______________________________

COMMON LIFE GOAL Personal Choice and Independence
PRIORITY (1 = HIGHEST, 10 = LOWEST) ☐
HOW I WILL MEET THIS GOAL (WHAT I WILL DO)
1. ______
2. ______
3. ______
4. ______
5. ______

COMMON LIFE GOAL Peace of Mind
PRIORITY (1 = HIGHEST, 10 = LOWEST) ☐
HOW I WILL MEET THIS GOAL (WHAT I WILL DO)
1. ______
2. ______
3. ______
4. ______
5. ______

Continued on next page

COMMON LIFE GOAL Relationships and Friendships

PRIORITY (1 = HIGHEST, 10 = LOWEST) ☐

HOW I WILL MEET THIS GOAL
(WHAT I WILL DO)

1. ______________________________
2. ______________________________
3. ______________________________
4. ______________________________
5. ______________________________

COMMON LIFE GOAL Community: Being Part of a Group

PRIORITY (1 = HIGHEST, 10 = LOWEST) ☐

HOW I WILL MEET THIS GOAL
(WHAT I WILL DO)

1. ______________________________
2. ______________________________
3. ______________________________
4. ______________________________
5. ______________________________

COMMON LIFE GOAL Spirituality: Having Meaning in Life

PRIORITY (1 = HIGHEST, 10 = LOWEST) ☐

HOW I WILL MEET THIS GOAL
(WHAT I WILL DO)

1. ____________________
2. ____________________
3. ____________________
4. ____________________
5. ____________________

COMMON LIFE GOAL Happiness

PRIORITY (1 = HIGHEST, 10 = LOWEST) ☐

HOW I WILL MEET THIS GOAL
(WHAT I WILL DO)

1. ____________________
2. ____________________
3. ____________________
4. ____________________
5. ____________________

Continued on next page

COMMON LIFE GOAL Creativity
PRIORITY (1 = HIGHEST, 10 = LOWEST) ☐
HOW I WILL MEET THIS GOAL (WHAT I WILL DO)
1. ____________________   2. ____________________   3. ____________________   4. ____________________   5. ____________________

Exercise 11.3: How I Will Know I Am Meeting My Goals

A person very often sets goals for himself but finds out later that those goals didn't work out as planned. Sometimes, this happens when it is too late and the person has already encountered problems. This difficulty happens because the person did not monitor himself and what was happening to him, so he missed important cues or signals that something was going wrong. Sometimes, this happens because he set goals that weren't realistic for him to try to achieve. Similarly, in order for you to have a good life plan that works for you, you need to know that you are meeting your goals. In this exercise, indicate for each goal and the specific activities in exercise 11.2 how you will know that you are meeting that goal. Please be specific.

COMMON LIFE GOAL	HOW I WILL KNOW I AM MEETING MY GOALS
Life: Living and Surviving	1. ______________________ ______________________ 2. ______________________ ______________________ 3. ______________________ ______________________ 4. ______________________ ______________________ 5. ______________________ ______________________
Knowledge: Learning and Knowing	1. ______________________ ______________________ 2. ______________________ ______________________ 3. ______________________ ______________________ 4. ______________________ ______________________ 5. ______________________ ______________________

Continued on next page

COMMON LIFE GOAL	HOW I WILL KNOW I AM MEETING MY GOALS
Being Good at Work and Play	1. ____________ ____________ 2. ____________ ____________ 3. ____________ ____________ 4. ____________ ____________ 5. ____________ ____________
Personal Choice and Independence	1. ____________ ____________ 2. ____________ ____________ 3. ____________ ____________ 4. ____________ ____________ 5. ____________ ____________

COMMON LIFE GOAL	HOW I WILL KNOW I AM MEETING MY GOALS
Peace of Mind	1. ____________________ ____________________ 2. ____________________ ____________________ 3. ____________________ ____________________ 4. ____________________ ____________________ 5. ____________________ ____________________
Relationships and Friendships	1. ____________________ ____________________ 2. ____________________ ____________________ 3. ____________________ ____________________ 4. ____________________ ____________________ 5. ____________________ ____________________

Continued on next page

COMMON LIFE GOAL	HOW I WILL KNOW I AM MEETING MY GOALS
Community: Being Part of a Group	1. ____________ ____________ 2. ____________ ____________ 3. ____________ ____________ 4. ____________ ____________ 5. ____________ ____________
Spirituality: Having Meaning in Life	1. ____________ ____________ 2. ____________ ____________ 3. ____________ ____________ 4. ____________ ____________ 5. ____________ ____________

COMMON LIFE GOAL	HOW I WILL KNOW I AM MEETING MY GOALS
Happiness	1. ____________ ____________ 2. ____________ ____________ 3. ____________ ____________ 4. ____________ ____________ 5. ____________ ____________
Creativity	1. ____________ ____________ 2. ____________ ____________ 3. ____________ ____________ 4. ____________ ____________ 5. ____________ ____________

Continued on next page

Exercise 11.4: How Others Will Know I Am Meeting My Goals

In addition to your being able to know whether or not you are meeting your goals, it is very important that others are also able to see whether you are achieving your goals. This awareness by others will be important because in order for you to have a good life and also to manage your risk, you will need to rely on support persons to help you. Sometimes you miss things that others notice and you need to rely on others for help. Also, when you are on supervision and/or getting treatment in the community, those who work with you will need to know if you are on track.

1. First, list here the people who are on your support team, including those who are on your case management team who are working with you in the community:

1. ______________________	6. ______________________
2. ______________________	7. ______________________
3. ______________________	8. ______________________
4. ______________________	9. ______________________
5. ______________________	10. ______________________

2. For this next part of the exercise, indicate how, for each of the common life goals, others will know you are meeting your goals. Describe what they will see about how you are feeling and what you are doing. It is very important to be very specific.

COMMON LIFE GOAL	HOW OTHERS WILL KNOW I AM MEETING MY GOALS
Life: Living and Surviving	1. ______ ______ 2. ______ ______ 3. ______ ______ 4. ______ ______ 5. ______ ______
Knowledge: Learning and Knowing	1. ______ ______ 2. ______ ______ 3. ______ ______ 4. ______ ______ 5. ______ ______

Continued on next page

COMMON LIFE GOAL	HOW OTHERS WILL KNOW I AM MEETING MY GOALS
Being Good at Work and Play	1. ____________________ ____________________ 2. ____________________ ____________________ 3. ____________________ ____________________ 4. ____________________ ____________________ 5. ____________________ ____________________
Personal Choice and Independence	1. ____________________ ____________________ 2. ____________________ ____________________ 3. ____________________ ____________________ 4. ____________________ ____________________ 5. ____________________ ____________________

COMMON LIFE GOAL	HOW OTHERS WILL KNOW I AM MEETING MY GOALS
Peace of Mind	1. ______ ______ 2. ______ ______ 3. ______ ______ 4. ______ ______ 5. ______ ______
Relationships and Friendships	1. ______ ______ 2. ______ ______ 3. ______ ______ 4. ______ ______ 5. ______ ______

Continued on next page

COMMON LIFE GOAL	HOW OTHERS WILL KNOW I AM MEETING MY GOALS
Community: Being Part of a Group	1. ______ ______ 2. ______ ______ 3. ______ ______ 4. ______ ______ 5. ______ ______
Spirituality: Having Meaning in Life	1. ______ ______ 2. ______ ______ 3. ______ ______ 4. ______ ______ 5. ______ ______

COMMON LIFE GOAL	HOW OTHERS WILL KNOW I AM MEETING MY GOALS
Happiness	1. ______________________ ______________________ 2. ______________________ ______________________ 3. ______________________ ______________________ 4. ______________________ ______________________ 5. ______________________ ______________________
Creativity	1. ______________________ ______________________ 2. ______________________ ______________________ 3. ______________________ ______________________ 4. ______________________ ______________________ 5. ______________________ ______________________

Continued on next page

Exercise 11.5: How I (and Others) Will Know That I Am Not Meeting My Goals

In the last two exercises, you indicated specific ways that you and others will know that you are meeting your goals and following your good life plan. Sometimes, despite your best intentions, events do not work out as planned. Often there are signs that this is happening, even if you are not always aware of these signs. If you have been in treatment programs that use relapse prevention plans, you have learned to recognize what are called "warning signs." These are signs that you or others would notice that indicate your risk to offend might be increasing. The exercise in this section is somewhat similar to this approach, except it focuses on signs that you might not be living your good life plan and meeting your life goals and that you may be having trouble managing your risk.

In the chart that follows, first indicate how you and others will know that you are not following your plan or that you not able to meet some of your goals. Next, describe what you will do in these situations. This exercise will provide you with a set of ideas that you can turn to if things start to go wrong. Last, indicate how problems implementing your good life plan are related to your risk factors. You may wish to review your work in exercise 4.2, in which you explored these links.

GOAL OF MY GOOD LIFE PLAN Life: Living and Surviving	
SIGNS THAT I MAY NOT BE GETTING WHAT IS IMPORTANT TO ME	WHAT I WILL DO
1. ______ ______	1. ______ ______
2. ______ ______	2. ______ ______
3. ______ ______	3. ______ ______
4. ______ ______	4. ______ ______
5. ______ ______	5. ______ ______

LINKS TO RISK AND RISK FACTORS
1. ______ ______
2. ______ ______
3. ______ ______
4. ______ ______
5. ______ ______

Continued on next page

GOAL OF MY GOOD LIFE PLAN Knowledge: Learning and Knowing	
SIGNS THAT I MAY NOT BE GETTING WHAT IS IMPORTANT TO ME	WHAT I WILL DO
1. ______ ______	1. ______ ______
2. ______ ______	2. ______ ______
3. ______ ______	3. ______ ______
4. ______ ______	4. ______ ______
5. ______ ______	5. ______ ______

LINKS TO RISK AND RISK FACTORS
1. ______ ______
2. ______ ______
3. ______ ______
4. ______ ______
5. ______ ______

GOAL OF MY GOOD LIFE PLAN Being Good at Work and Play	
SIGNS THAT I MAY NOT BE GETTING WHAT IS IMPORTANT TO ME	WHAT I WILL DO
1. ______ ______	1. ______ ______
2. ______ ______	2. ______ ______
3. ______ ______	3. ______ ______
4. ______ ______	4. ______ ______
5. ______ ______	5. ______ ______
LINKS TO RISK AND RISK FACTORS	
1. ______ ______	
2. ______ ______	
3. ______ ______	
4. ______ ______	
5. ______ ______	

Continued on next page

GOAL OF MY GOOD LIFE PLAN Personal Choice and Independence	
SIGNS THAT I MAY NOT BE GETTING WHAT IS IMPORTANT TO ME	WHAT I WILL DO
1. ____________________ ____________________	1. ____________________ ____________________
2. ____________________ ____________________	2. ____________________ ____________________
3. ____________________ ____________________	3. ____________________ ____________________
4. ____________________ ____________________	4. ____________________ ____________________
5. ____________________ ____________________	5. ____________________ ____________________

LINKS TO RISK AND RISK FACTORS
1. ____ ____
2. ____ ____
3. ____ ____
4. ____ ____
5. ____ ____

GOAL OF MY GOOD LIFE PLAN Peace of Mind	
SIGNS THAT I MAY NOT BE GETTING WHAT IS IMPORTANT TO ME	WHAT I WILL DO
1. ______ ______	1. ______ ______
2. ______ ______	2. ______ ______
3. ______ ______	3. ______ ______
4. ______ ______	4. ______ ______
5. ______ ______	5. ______ ______

LINKS TO RISK AND RISK FACTORS
1. ______ ______
2. ______ ______
3. ______ ______
4. ______ ______
5. ______ ______

Continued on next page

GOAL OF MY GOOD LIFE PLAN Relationships and Friendships	
SIGNS THAT I MAY NOT BE GETTING WHAT IS IMPORTANT TO ME	WHAT I WILL DO
1. ________________	1. ________________
________________	________________
2. ________________	2. ________________
________________	________________
3. ________________	3. ________________
________________	________________
4. ________________	4. ________________
________________	________________
5. ________________	5. ________________
________________	________________

LINKS TO RISK AND RISK FACTORS
1. ________________
____
2. ________________
____
3. ________________
____
4. ________________
____
5. ________________
____

GOAL OF MY GOOD LIFE PLAN Community: Being Part of a Group	
SIGNS THAT I MAY NOT BE GETTING WHAT IS IMPORTANT TO ME	**WHAT I WILL DO**
1. ______	1. ______
2. ______	2. ______
3. ______	3. ______
4. ______	4. ______
5. ______	5. ______

LINKS TO RISK AND RISK FACTORS
1. ______
2. ______
3. ______
4. ______
5. ______

Continued on next page

GOAL OF MY GOOD LIFE PLAN Spirituality: Having Meaning in Life

SIGNS THAT I MAY NOT BE GETTING WHAT IS IMPORTANT TO ME	WHAT I WILL DO
1. ______	1. ______
2. ______	2. ______
3. ______	3. ______
4. ______	4. ______
5. ______	5. ______

LINKS TO RISK AND RISK FACTORS
1. ______
2. ______
3. ______
4. ______
5. ______

GOAL OF MY GOOD LIFE PLAN Happiness	
SIGNS THAT I MAY NOT BE GETTING WHAT IS IMPORTANT TO ME	WHAT I WILL DO
1. ______ ______	1. ______ ______
2. ______ ______	2. ______ ______
3. ______ ______	3. ______ ______
4. ______ ______	4. ______ ______
5. ______ ______	5. ______ ______

LINKS TO RISK AND RISK FACTORS
1. ______ ______
2. ______ ______
3. ______ ______
4. ______ ______
5. ______ ______

Continued on next page

GOAL OF MY GOOD LIFE PLAN Creativity	
SIGNS THAT I MAY NOT BE GETTING WHAT IS IMPORTANT TO ME	WHAT I WILL DO
1. ______	1. ______
2. ______	2. ______
3. ______	3. ______
4. ______	4. ______
5. ______	5. ______

LINKS TO RISK AND RISK FACTORS
1. ______
2. ______
3. ______
4. ______
5. ______

Exercise 11.6: Anticipating Problems (Flaws in My Good Life Plan)

In the last exercise, you indicated how others will know when you are not following your good life plan, and you also included the links between your good life plan and your risk factors. This next exercise looks in detail at the four specific problems or flaws in your plan, which you identified in chapter 2 and again in chapter 8. In this exercise, indicate how you and others will know that specific problems (the flaws) are occurring. Next, describe what you will do in these situations. Last, indicate whether these problems are linked to your risk factors and how they are linked.

Continued on next page

FUTURE POSSIBLE PROBLEMS (FLAWS) Means: How I Am Meeting My Goals	
THIS MAY BE HAPPENING	**WHAT I WILL DO**
1. ______________________	1. ______________________
______________________	______________________
2. ______________________	2. ______________________
______________________	______________________
3. ______________________	3. ______________________
______________________	______________________
4. ______________________	4. ______________________
______________________	______________________
5. ______________________	5. ______________________
______________________	______________________

LINKS TO RISK AND RISK FACTORS
1. ____
____
2. ____
____
3. ____
____
4. ____
____
5. ____
____

FUTURE POSSIBLE PROBLEMS (FLAWS) Too Narrow a Good Life Plan (Scope): When I Am Focusing Too Much on One or Only a Few Goals	
THIS MAY BE HAPPENING	**WHAT I WILL DO**
1. ____________________ ____________________	1. ____________________ ____________________
2. ____________________ ____________________	2. ____________________ ____________________
3. ____________________ ____________________	3. ____________________ ____________________
4. ____________________ ____________________	4. ____________________ ____________________
5. ____________________ ____________________	5. ____________________ ____________________

LINKS TO RISK AND RISK FACTORS
1. ____ ____
2. ____ ____
3. ____ ____
4. ____ ____
5. ____ ____

Continued on next page

FUTURE POSSIBLE PROBLEMS (FLAWS)	Conflict Between Goals: When My Goals Are Not Aligned with Each Other
THIS MAY BE HAPPENING	**WHAT I WILL DO**
1. ______	1. ______
2. ______	2. ______
3. ______	3. ______
4. ______	4. ______
5. ______	5. ______

LINKS TO RISK AND RISK FACTORS

1. ______
2. ______
3. ______
4. ______
5. ______

FUTURE POSSIBLE PROBLEMS (FLAWS) Lack of Skills: When I Don't Have or Use My Skills	
THIS MAY BE HAPPENING	**WHAT I WILL DO**
1. ______ ______	1. ______ ______
2. ______ ______	2. ______ ______
3. ______ ______	3. ______ ______
4. ______ ______	4. ______ ______
5. ______ ______	5. ______ ______

LINKS TO RISK AND RISK FACTORS
1. ______ ______
2. ______ ______
3. ______ ______
4. ______ ______
5. ______ ______

Continued on next page

FUTURE POSSIBLE PROBLEMS (FLAWS) Lack of Opportunities: When Problems in My Environment Interfere in My Goals	
THIS MAY BE HAPPENING	WHAT I WILL DO
1. ______	1. ______
2. ______	2. ______
3. ______	3. ______
4. ______	4. ______
5. ______	5. ______

LINKS TO RISK AND RISK FACTORS
1. ______
2. ______
3. ______
4. ______
5. ______

Exercise 11.7: Putting My Good Life Plan Together

The final exercise in this section is to put your good life plan together in the table provided on the next pages. You have already done the vast majority of the work in this section of the workbook. As you put these pieces together and look at them all in one place, ask yourself: How does this look now that I can actually see it all put together? What pieces might be missing? Are there parts of earlier exercises to which I should return?

Continued on next page

My Good Life Plan Summary

COMMON LIFE GOAL	HOW I WILL MEET THIS GOAL	HOW I AND OTHERS WILL KNOW I AM MEETING THIS GOAL
Life: Living and Surviving		
Knowledge: Learning and Knowing		
Being Good at Work and Play		
Personal Choice and Independence		
Peace of Mind		
Relationships and Friendships		
Community: Being Part of a Group		
Spirituality: Having Meaning in Life		
Happiness		
Creativity		

PROBLEMS I WILL NEED TO MANAGE (FLAWS)	RISK FACTORS RELATED TO THIS GOAL	WARNING SIGNS FOR RISK (HOW I AND OTHERS WILL KNOW)	HOW I WILL USE SELF-REGULATION SKILLS AND STRATEGIES

Summary

In this part of the workbook you have explored your plan for a good life and the important goals that you have. You have reviewed how you and others will know that you are being successful. You have also explored specific possible problems implementing your good life plan, and—most importantly—you have assembled a way for yourself and others to recognize when your plan is working and when it is not working. Congratulations! You have just developed your good life plan! The final part of the workbook focuses on how to be successful in the community.

CHAPTER 12

In the Community

During or after treatment, it is possible that you will participate in a different program for follow-up or maintenance and will be under supervision by a parole or probation officer in the community. Because treatment programs are different from one place to another, your follow-up and supervision may not be focused on treatment that involves having a good life, or even on the self-regulation approach. In fact, some people working with you will be relying on a relapse prevention model because they are most familiar with this approach. For example, your parole officer may ask you about your *relapse prevention plan*. Basically what he or she means is your risk management plan and your self-regulation strategies. But, he or she may not be familiar with the concept of a good life plan. So you may need to explain your plan to him or her and show how it links with your plans to manage your risk. Similarly, your family and friends may not understand what a good life plan is and how it can help you to manage your risk to re-offend.

Even if the people in your community team use the good life approach to treatment, they will want to know from you what your good life plan is and what it means. In this part of the workbook, you will be asked to consider ways to explain your good life plan to people who may not be familiar with it. You have already developed your good life plan and your risk management plan (chapters 10 and 11), so what you will do in this last part of this workbook is to think about how you can explain these elements to others so they can work with you and help you. Your ability to explain your plan to others also helps you look at how to implement your plan in the community, and what to do if your plan does not go as you expect.

Explaining your plan to others can be helpful to you for a number of reasons. First, the people in your life will be better able to help you achieve your plan. Second, the more you explain your plan, the better they will understand it. And finally, the more practice you have explaining your plan, the better *you* will understand it and apply it.

Changing My Good Life Plan

As you learned in chapter 2, it is important that your good life plan be something that is realistic for you and something you can actually practice in your community. Having goals in your plan that you won't be able to achieve will just lead to frustration and to a life that is not balanced or satisfying—and it can also lead to an increased risk for re-offending! You have worked very hard to reach this point in treatment. Know that sometimes in life, things do not work out as people plan them, or restrictions get in the way of meeting goals. If you find that when you are in the community, your plan isn't working, it is *extremely important* that you tell your community team and your support people. In chapter 11, you talked about signs you and others can recognize that tell you and others that you are meeting your goals and signs that you might be having trouble. People on your support team need to know about these things so they can help you as soon as you start to have any difficulties at all.

You may need to make some changes to your good life plan, but it is *extremely* important that you do not make these changes on your own! If you are having any difficulties meeting your goals and implementing your plan, talk to your community team and support people right away and have them help you make any changes or develop a "Plan B." Bringing in others to help you will increase your chances of meeting your goals effectively and will help you to not go back to old, problematic ways.

Exercise 12.1: In the Community

1. Who are the people on your community management team:

1. ________________	5. ________________
2. ________________	6. ________________
3. ________________	7. ________________
4. ________________	8. ________________

2. Who are the additional supports you have in the community (e.g., family, friends, employer, religious leader, etc.)

1. ________________	5. ________________
2. ________________	6. ________________
3. ________________	7. ________________
4. ________________	8. ________________

3. Where will you be living?

____

4. Where will you be working?

____

5. What are five strengths you have that it will be good for others to know about?

   1. ____
   2. ____
   3. ____
   4. ____
   5. ____

6. What are five things about your motivation to stay safe in the community that others should know so that they can best support you?

   1. ____
   2. ____
   3. ____
   4. ____
   5. ____

7. What restrictions do you have?

____

____

____

____

8. What are five warning signs that would indicate it is time for your community management team to take action?

   1. ____
   2. ____
   3. ____
   4. ____
   5. ____

Exercise 12.2: Explaining My Good Life Plan

1. How would you describe the *idea* of a good life plan to someone who did not know what it was? What would you tell that person about why, in treatment, a good life plan is important? How would you explain its purpose or purposes? How would you explain why people develop a good life plan?

2. Now think about the specific elements of a good life plan. How would you describe the 10 common life goals to someone who did not know what these were?

   Life (Living and Surviving):

   Knowledge (Learning and Knowing):

   Being Good at Work and Play:

Personal Choice and Independence:

Peace of Mind:

Relationships and Friendships:

Community (Being Part of a Group):

Spirituality (Having Meaning in Life):

Happiness:

Creativity:

3. How would you explain why it is important to have these positive goals in your life?

4. How would you explain what happens when people don't have these positive goals in their lives?

5. How would you explain what could happen for you if *you* don't have these positive goals in your life?

6. How would you explain how other people can help you to get these positive goals in your life?

______

______

______

______

______

______

7. How would you explain the relationship between meeting these positive goals and reducing your risk to re-offend?

______

______

______

______

______

______

8. Next, think about the five flaws or problems that can happen when people try to implement their good life plans. How would you explain each of these flaws to someone who did not know what they were? How would you explain what happens when these flaws or problems happen?

   Ways to Meet Goals (Means):

   ______

   ______

   ______

   Too Narrow a Good Life Plan (Scope):

   ______

   ______

   ______

Conflict Between Goals:

Lack of Skills:

Lack of Opportunities:

9. How would you explain how *your own problems or flaws* could affect your good life plan?

Ways to Meet Goals (Means):

Too Narrow a Good Life Plan (Scope):

Conflict Between Goals:

Lack of Skills:

____

____

____

Lack of Opportunities:

____

____

____

10. How would you explain how other people can help you to cope with these flaws or problems?

____

____

____

____

____

____

Exercise 12.3:
Explaining My Risk Management Plan

1. How would you describe the *idea* of a risk management plan to someone who did not know what it was? What would you tell them about why, in treatment, people develop this plan? How would you explain what its purpose or purposes are? How would you explain why *you* developed a risk management plan?

____

____

____

____

____

____

2. This next question is a little harder: How would you explain to someone the relationship between a good life plan and a risk management plan? How would you describe what is similar about the plans and what is different about them?

____

____

____

____

____

____

3. How would you explain what risk factors are and how they increase a person's chances of offending and re-offending?

____

____

____

____

____

____

4. How would you explain your own risk factors?

____

____

____

____

____

____

5. How would you explain the skills and strategies you have learned to manage your risk factors?

____

____

6. How would you explain to other people how they can help you use your skills and strategies to manage your risk factors?

Exercise 12.4: Explaining My Self-Regulation and My Offense Pathway

1. How would you explain the *idea* of self-regulation to someone who did not know what it was? How would you explain the three different self-regulation styles?

   Under-Regulation:

   Mis-Regulation:

Controlled Regulation:

____

____

____

2. How would you explain your own self-regulation style to someone who did not know what it was?

____

____

____

____

____

____

3. How would you explain the relationship between your self-regulation style and meeting your life goals? How would you explain when your self-regulation helps you meet your goals and when it results in problems or offending?

____

____

____

____

____

____

4. How would you explain the relationship between your own self-regulation style and your offending?

____

____

____

____

____

____

5. What would you tell the people in your life about how you have managed your behavior in the past, what new strategies and skills you have learned, and how those people can help you with your self-regulation?

6. How would you explain the *idea* of offense pathways to someone who did not know what they were?

7. How would you explain the idea of each of the four offense pathways to someone who did not know what they were?

   Avoidant-Passive Pathway:

   Avoidant-Active Pathway:

   Approach-Automatic Pathway:

Approach-Explicit Pathway:

____

____

____

8. How would you explain your own offense pathway or pathways to someone who did not know what your pathway was? What would you tell them about what happens?

____

____

____

____

____

____

____

9. How would you explain the skills and strategies you have learned to manage your offense pathway(s)?

____

____

____

____

____

____

____

10. How would you explain how other people will see if you are at risk or if an offense chain is triggered for you?

____

____

____

____

11. How would you explain how other people can help you if they thought you were at risk or if an offense chain is triggered for you?

Exercise 12.5: Putting It All Together

This last exercise is not really an exercise for this workbook. It is more of an additional resource for your understanding. Usually, when you change to another treatment program or you go into supervision for the first time, you will be asked to explain who you are, what your risk management plans are, and, in this case, what your good life plan is. The previous exercises were designed to help you think about how you might explain to other people all of the different things you've learned, whether they are family, friends, partners, bosses, or people on your community team.

In order for people to be aware of everything they need to know so they can help and support you, you should share the good life plan and risk management plan that you did in chapters 10 and 11 with them. In those two parts, you developed very specific strategies that you will use to implement these plans. You also looked at how both you and other people will know if you are effectively implementing your plans and if and when you are having difficulty. It is important that other people in your life have an in-depth awareness of all of this information in order to help you to be successful. On the next two pages, you will find a chart that you can use to summarize the work you have done in this workbook and so you and others can have an at-a-glance understanding of your plans. This summary is optional for you but, whether or not you use it, you should share your specific plans with everyone in your life.

My Plans at a Glance

COMMON LIFE GOAL	WAYS TO MEET GOALS (MEANS)	HOW I WILL KNOW I AM MEETING THESE GOALS
Life: Living and Surviving		
Knowledge: Learning and Knowing		
Being Good at Work and Play		
Personal Choice and Independence		
Peace of Mind		
Relationships and Friendships		
Community: Being Part of a Group		
Spirituality: Having Meaning in Life		
Happiness		
Creativity		

HOW OTHERS WILL KNOW I AM MEETING MY GOALS	FLAWS OR PROBLEMS I WILL NEED TO MANAGE	HOW OTHERS WILL KNOW I AM NOT MEETING MY GOALS (WARNING SIGNS)	HOW OTHERS WILL KNOW I AM NOT MANAGING MY RISKS (WARNING SIGNS)

Summary

Congratulations on completing this workbook. Your efforts are an excellent start toward living a healthy, safe, and satisfying life in the community. You have explored your good life plans in the past and present and developed a plan for your future. You have examined your life and the factors that led to your goals and who you are today, as well as your risk factors, sexual offenses, offense chain, and offense pathway in detail. Most important of all, you have established plans for building a better life and managing your risk to re-offend. Hopefully, you will have accomplished many aspects of this work that are specific and important to you and have developed ways to implement your plan and stay motivated to make important changes to your life. The plans you've developed might include topics that have not been covered in this book, such as making amends to people you have hurt or addressing issues related to education, substance use, or mental health. All of these details play a part in your good life plan and in managing your risk. We hope you pursue a better life to the best of your abilities and wish you the very best in all of these endeavors!